How to be an Outstanding Primary Teaching Assistant

How to be an Outstanding Primary Teaching Assistant

Emma Davie

BLOOMSBURY

LONDON · OXFORD · NEW YORK · NEW DELHI · SYDNEY

Bloomsbury Education
An imprint of Bloomsbury Publishing Plc

50 Bedford Square	1385 Broadway
London	New York
WC1B 3DP	NY 10018
UK	USA

www.bloomsbury.com

BLOOMSBURY and the Diana logo are trademarks of Bloomsbury Publishing Plc

First published in Great Britain 2017

A catalogue record for this book is available from the British Library.

ISBN
PB: 9781472934611
ePub: 9781472934635
ePDF: 9781472934628

Library of Congress Cataloguing-in-Publication data has been applied for.

2 4 6 8 10 9 7 5 3 1

Typeset by Newgen Knowledge Works Pvt. Ltd., Chennai, India
Printed and bound in Great Britain by CPI Group (UK) Ltd, Croydon CR0 4YY

This book is produced using paper that is made from wood grown in managed,
sustainable forests. It is natural, renewable and recyclable. The logging and
manufacturing processes conform to the environmental regulations of the
country of origin.

To find out more about our authors and books visit www.bloomsbury.com.
Here you will find extracts, author interviews, details of forthcoming events
and the option to sign up for our newsletters.

Contents

Acknowledgements

I have so many people to thank for taking me on this amazing journey; it feels a little bit like I am writing an Oscar speech, so here goes...

First of all I would like to thank my lovely husband of 21 years, Jason, for always looking after me, supporting me no matter what mad things I decide to do. I would also like to thank my two beautiful children: Joshua (21) and Jack (13) who have both inspired me to write this book and make me proud every single day. Special thanks need to go to my mum, dad and brother for always being there to support me; it really is appreciated.

I would, of course, like to thank all of the SMT at my current school for giving me the time and support to follow my dreams. SR and GS, I really do thank you from the bottom of my heart. I could not do my job at all without all of my fellow TAs, learning mentors and teachers. So, Julie and Claire, thank you for always being there to lend a supportive ear (and give me a hug or three!).

I also want to thank my friend, Laura, as she has read through every word of this book to make sure I have not missed anything out and has always been at the end of the phone if I need anything (and I do mean *anything*).

The amazing lecturers from University College Birmingham (UCB) also deserve a special mention, as they have all inspired me to question my practice every day. Marj Jeavons, Helen Mortimer, Alison Williams, Nicola Sperrin, Gez Teager and Claire Largin – thank you so much.

And last, but not least, I would like to thank the amazing editors at Bloomsbury Publishing. First of all – a big thank you to Holly Gardner, who first invited me to write my very first book, and, of course, my editor, Miriam Davey. You have always been at the end of the phone, answered my emails when I was not sure what to do and motivated me when I thought I could not reach the finish line, so for that I am eternally grateful.

I know I have many more people to be grateful to, but I do have a word limit! So, thank you to everyone who has supported me. I really am very lucky!

Introduction

Now I am actually writing this book, I am filled with all kinds of emotions; I am excited and apprehensive at the same time. Excited, as I have never had the opportunity to sit down and think about what my job as a teaching assistant (TA) entails. I have never taken the time to question my practice, to think about what impact being a TA has on me every day and what impact I have on the children I support. But also very apprehensive, as you might not like the book and think you have wasted your hard-earned money.

When I first became a TA (17 years ago) my role was very different to what it is now; it was far more about making sure the classroom was ready for lessons to take place and about assisting the teacher in the class. However, over the last ten years, the role and responsibilities of the role have steadily grown and the amount of time spent actually working with the children has risen dramatically (which is obviously a good thing, as the children are the main reason we want to be TAs). However, now the new National Curriculum and *Special Educational Needs and Disability Code of Practice* have come into effect (in September 2014) the role of a TA has changed again. As a TA working under the new guidelines you are now expected to spend much of the day supporting children and enabling them to access the new curriculum, especially those children with special educational needs and disability (SEND), English as an additional language (EAL) and behavioural difficulties. However, the role still requires you to support children to develop both socially and emotionally, to deal with any issues that may prevent the child from making the progress expected and record any improvements made by the children, as well as all of the other tasks previously carried out.

The aim of this book is to give you an honest and true reflection of what you could be asked to do during a normal school day. One of the first skills that will be tested in your role as a TA is the ability to be flexible and be able to change between the many different roles you will take on during a working day (don't worry – these are all included in Chapter 1). At times, the stresses of the job can seem overwhelming, but there will always be people in the setting who will be there to support you, as you are not just joining a place of work, you are also joining a 'family'. There will always be a TA (or three) who will share their experiences with you. I suppose that is one of the other reasons I decided to write this book. I have been lucky enough to work alongside many talented, creative and clever TAs over the years, who have passed on many different skills that can be used to support a child. So as well as letting you know what it is like to be a TA, I am hopefully going to give you lots of practical ideas and strategies that may help you to meet the needs of the children (whatever these may be), either individual children or small groups, as well as saving you precious time. So read, enjoy and be 'outstanding'...

Chapter 1
The role of the teaching assistant

If you are reading this, you are probably either training to become a teaching assistant or you have already gained your qualification. Whichever one it is, well done you! People who do not work in education often do not realise how difficult it can be to work with children all day, every day. It can very emotionally and physically demanding and, believe me, no two days are the same. When you tell people you work in a school, you often hear comments like, 'Your job is easy. All you do is sit down all day and read with the children.' 'It must be really hard having all of the holidays you have.' I have heard them all over the last 17 years, but none of them make me love my job any less. I could not imagine myself doing anything else. I hope reading this book will help to provide you with some time-saving ideas and practical advice that will help you to support children of all ages and abilities, but, above all, become an 'outstanding teaching assistant'.

All the way through this book the term 'teaching assistant' (TA) is going to be used many times; this can be used to cover learning support staff (LSS), classroom assistants (CAs), support staff and higher level teaching assistants (HLTAs). The first thing I want to let you know is that the role of a teaching assistant can vary massively from school to school; in some schools the TAs can make tea and coffee for staff, mix paint and set up the classroom for the forthcoming activities. However, over the last few years certainly, there has been far more responsibility placed on the TAs to support the teaching and learning of the children. You need to be clear about what is and is not part of your job, so get out that job description and study it! All of these responsibilities, of course, will depend on the grade of teaching assistant that you have qualified at and, of course, your pay scale. The best way to clarify any issues with expectations is to talk to the teacher that you work with and your line manager: either your year group leader, phase leader or a member of SMT (senior management team). By doing this, you can make sure that the expectations of you are clear from the outset and any misconceptions are quickly dealt with. The relationship you build up with the teacher you work alongside will have a huge impact on how well the classroom runs, but, more importantly, how the children learn. Children only learn when they are confident and happy, and that comes from the learning environment set by the adults – you!

The role of the teaching assistant, as I have already said, has changed immensely over the years and very much depends on the government in power. These changes will continue, now that the new National Curriculum and SEN Code of Practice have come into effect. The magnitude and speed with which these changes were brought in have been controversial and caused much uncertainty in schools across the country.

In addition to your official role as a TA, throughout the day you will be required to take on a variety of different roles, many of which have not featured in any teaching assistant course I have heard of. During any given day it may be necessary to be: a teacher, carer, police officer, counsellor, secretary, first aider, interior designer, referee, mathematician, linguist and, most importantly, a positive role model, to name but a few. By mastering and learning to juggle these roles, you will ensure that the children in your care are happy and ready to learn.

This chapter is hopefully going to provide some really simple, practical ideas on how all of these roles can be juggled successfully.

Classroom organisation (secretary)

Within any given week you will work with many different children, all requiring help or support to varying degrees, whether they are a child with special educational needs and disability (SEND), with English as an additional language (EAL) or gifted and talented (G and T). Being organised and managing your time effectively is definitely the key to success and will make your working day far easier.

Resources

Every day, a variety of resources will be needed for each lesson. One of the most effective ways to ensure these are ready is to work alongside the teacher during the planning process. Knowing what is going on, and when, will not only enhance the children's teaching and learning, but will also enable you to know what needs to be prepared: worksheets, resources, etc. It will also enable you and the teacher to have a discussion about realistic timescales for these tasks to be completed.

Tips

Tip 1: Have an IN and OUT tray so that you know what tasks you have to complete within the day and the jobs that can wait until later. Doing tasks ahead of time stops the stress of doing them at the last minute: *make sure you stay ahead!*

Tip 2: Make sure you have a stash of sticky notes to mark each piece of photocopying or laminating, so that you do not forget how many copies are required. The photocopier and laminator will soon become your best friends in school.

Tip 3: Get to know the resource manager as soon as possible, as he/she will be the fount of all knowledge when it comes to whether there is a certain resource available in school, or whether it will need to be ordered.

Letters

An important part of school life is keeping parents informed about what is happening within the setting, encouraging them to be involved in their child's education and to become part of the school community. One of the most effective ways to do this is through letters. Believe me, there is not a day that goes by without a letter or three being given out. Some of the letters that may be sent out include:

- Newsletters – help to keep parents informed of important up-and-coming events for their diary.

- Home/school agreements – will help ensure continuity between home and school, by highlighting the importance of good attendance, punctuality, homework and appropriate use of digital devices.

- Parents' evening letters – invite parents into school, to discuss their children's achievements, academic attainment and areas for improvement, if needed.

- Trip letters – let parents know about forthcoming trips that have been booked to support their learning and understanding about a particular topic. The letter will give details about: the time and date of the trip, the cost to the parent, the clothing needed and the packed lunch details; it will also allow the setting to gain consent for the child to go on the trip.

- Head lice letters – inform parents that a child in the class has head lice and give advice and tips on how to prevent head lice from spreading further.

- Inspire courses letters – offer parents the chance to come into school to work alongside their child, which, in turn, promotes home/school learning.

- School fair letters – ask parents to come and support the setting's fundraising initiatives.

- Charity day letters – encourage parents to get involved in fundraising and supporting a charity in the wider community.

- Food tasting letters – notify parents of a food-tasting activity, so that parental consent may be given (as there are now so many children with different allergies or food intolerances).

- After-school club letters have two functions: the first is to invite children to attend a club after school hours, such as football or language club; the second is to gain the parental consent needed for the child to be able to go to the club.

Tips

Tip 1: Keep a couple of extra copies of any letters that have been sent out to parents. It will save you time when searching for a master copy if a child loses their copy. Better yet, keep a spare ten copies!

Tip 2: Make phone calls to parents as soon as you know a child has forgotten to bring in a consent slip or letter. This will ensure the child will not feel worried throughout the day about them not being able to participate in the activity.

> **Tip 3:** Keep a list of which children attend which clubs and on what days, especially if working with younger children, as they are likely to forget.

Money

Within all primary school settings children are often required to bring in money for dinners, snacks, trips and photographs. Having a system that works for the collection of money is an important part of your job, as it ensures that the children receive what they have paid for. In many settings, it is now part of the TA's role to collect in any monies that the children bring into school, to record the amount brought in by each child, and to send it down to the office. However, in smaller settings, parents can only pay money into the office. More and more schools are now trialling cashless systems in settings, so that any discrepancies can be kept to a minimum. So, I suggest that you check what the policy is on collecting money in your setting (this again is something that you can ask your colleagues).

Tips

Tip 1: Make a record of all the children that have paid for a snack, both on your own class list and on the record sent to the office, as this will help if any discrepancies arise.

(I have had a child, on more than one occasion, spend their snack money or dinner money in the local shop and then tell the parents the money has been paid to the school.)

Tip 2: Send out reminder slips if a child has not paid their dinner or snack money, so that arrears do not build up.

Planning

Part of the role of a TA may be to plan activities for small intervention groups, depending on the setting you work in. In order to do this effectively, the first port of call would definitely be the special (educational) needs coordinator (SENCo) or special educational needs disability coordinator (SENDCo) as they will have a comprehensive overview of the children and their needs (whatever these may be). I would also suggest some 'light bedtime reading' of the SEN folder. This is an invaluable tool, as it will be able to tell you about the specific medical and/or learning needs the children in your class have. This information is crucial, as it will help you when supporting the children, both inside and outside the classroom.

Another important resource when planning lessons or activities is the parents. We have all heard the cliché 'nobody knows the child like the parents do'. But it is true. Parents can provide you with so much information about their child (much more than is written in any folder). The information given by parents can make a real difference to the child and their experience of school life. Such information could include:

- The likes and dislikes of the child.

- What motivates and encourages the child to participate in their learning.

- The most effective strategies used to reward and praise the child (stickers, computer time and football are the most popular in our setting).

- What triggers behavioural issues.

- How to soothe and calm the child.

Tips

Tip 1: Have a copy of the planning on the wall, so that the children know what they are doing. This will also help if you are ever off ill and someone needs to step into your shoes.

Tip 2: Annotate the planning after a lesson has finished. This will help you remember which activities have been successful and which ones may need tweaking, should you repeat it in the future.

Tip 3: Keep a digital copy of your planning and associated worksheets, as these can sometimes be reused for other groups you may work with. (There is no point reinventing the wheel.)

Tip 4: Have a resource column on your planning sheet. This will save you a huge amount of time when trying to remember which resources are needed for the week ahead.

Tip 5: Plan work around their areas of interest to encourage and motivate children to be involved in their learning.

Monday	Tuesday	Wednesday	Thursday	Friday	Resources needed

There will be times when you think you have tried everything with a particular child, and nothing you try will ever work again. I know I have! If and when this happens (and believe me it will) it is important that you ask for help from your colleagues, whether this be the SENDCo, the teacher or other teaching assistants who have been doing the job for many years. Colleagues will not only be able to provide you with support when you feel helpless, but also share a wealth of practical ideas, which will enable you to meet the needs of the children and motivate the children to become more involved in their learning. Take advantage of those colleagues who are often described as 'part of the furniture', as they are bound to have an idea or two (or three).

Do not worry: later chapters in this book offer further strategies and practical advice about working with small groups and working with children with SEN.

Marking

In some schools TAs are not required to mark work and make comments in books, but if you are expected to carry out marking, then please be aware that different schools have different marking policies. So, before marking any of the completed work, make sure you read the setting's marking policy. The policy will be able to:

- Advise you of the pen colour needed to mark any work the children have produced (most schools *do not* allow the use of red pen to make comments about children's work).

- Provide you with the codes you may need to use if children are required to make corrections or changes to their work, e.g. spelling error (SP), incorrect grammar (Gr) and missing punctuation (P).

- Tell you the symbols needed to show whether the child has completed their work independently (I), whether they required any adult help to complete the task (AH) or whether the teacher or TA has provided any verbal feedback to the child (VF).

- Describe how marking is used to inform the children of the next steps for learning. This is an important part of marking, as it sets out clearly what steps the children need to include in their next piece of work in order for improvements to be made.

In the setting I currently work in, we use the 'two stars and a wish' marking strategy and now know from speaking to other colleagues from other settings that this is used extensively in many other settings. The 'two stars' relate to two positive comments the marker can make about the work the child has completed. For example, the work was: well punctuated; beautifully presented; used an imaginative word; or positively linked to the learning objective. The 'wish' gives the marker the opportunity to suggest one change the child could make in the next piece of work in order to improve it in some way: check spellings or punctuation; rewrite a sentence; or, of course, reread their work and check it makes sense.

Funny story

Over the years I have used the 'two stars and a wish' marking strategy many times. The first few times I used it, nothing happened; but once the children got used to it, I started to get responses from the children in my group. These have included: 'I'm glad you enjoyed reading my work' and 'Thanks for reading my work.' I have also received a comment back when I have asked for speech marks to be included in the next piece of work: 'I will try and include speech marks next time, Miss – don't worry.'

These comments not only made me smile but also let me know the child had read the feedback I had given about their work.

Tips

Tip 1: Always keep a pen close at hand (ideally the one that has a blue, red, green and black nib). This way you will always be able to make a comment on work as and when needed.

EXTRA SPECIAL TIP: A great way to accumulate pens is to attend education shows, which are held at various venues around the country each year. The stall holders give away free pens.

Tip 2: Be positive and honest with your feedback. Talk to the child about why you have given the comment, whether this is good or bad. Either way, the child will remember these points in the future and include them in the next piece of work.

Tip 3: Do not be afraid to tell children what their next steps for learning are (to add punctuation, more adventurous words and new vocabulary). Children will soon start to see that these small changes can make a huge difference to their finished piece of work.

Tip 4: When marking a child's work, try to ensure you comment when a child has acted upon your previous comments. Noticing their progress and praising them explicitly for this is always a good motivator. Never underestimate the power of verbal praise!

Tip 5: Use stampers or small stickers in books to indicate when the work has been completed successfully, as some children love flicking through their books to see how many rewards they have in total.

As well as marking, planning and preparation (of some description) are now becoming part of being a TA, although as I have already mentioned, the expectation varies immensely between settings. If these tasks are part of your role, it may be necessary for the setting to arrange a specific time in your timetable when this can happen. This is sometimes called planning, preparation and assessment (PPA) time; this is time spent away from children (non-contact time) where you can mark books, gather resources and plan activities that can be used with the individual children or small intervention groups you support.

First aid (nurse)

Part of your role as a TA may require you to carry out a first-aid duty during the week and, again, is dependent on the setting. During break times and dinnertimes, you may be responsible for administering first aid to children for minor ailments such as head bumps, grazes to elbows and knees, and nose bleeds, etc. If not experienced or trained to carry out first aid, then it may be necessary to shadow a more experienced TA in order to see how accidents are dealt with and recorded in your setting. However, it may be necessary to attend a basic first-aid course to enhance your skills. But don't worry; this will be arranged by the setting and form part of your continued professional development (CPD).

Tips

Tip 1: Fill in an accident slip for any child that comes to you for first aid. This will cover you in the blame/claim society that we are in at present.

Tip 2: *Do not* be afraid to seek a second opinion if you are in any doubt.

Tip 3: If a child has a head bump or a visible mark, then seek the advice of a qualified first aider or a member of the senior leadership team (SLT) to see if a phone call needs to be made to the parents.

Tip 4: Make a note of the full name and class of the child who has come to first aid, so that the office can make the phone call to parents to inform them about an accident or injury their child has sustained. (It is sometimes easy to forget that there may be other children in the school with the same name as the child.)

Tip 5: Remember that you are only giving your opinion on any injury sustained by a child in your setting – you are not a medical practitioner or an X-ray machine. (I was once told this by our school nurse.)

As well as administering first aid following an accident, you may be working in a class to support or work alongside a child who has a specific medical need. Therefore, it may be necessary to undertake a more specific first-aid course. (Again, this will be arranged by the setting.) There are many courses you could attend, but the most common are: paediatric first aid; basic first aid; and first aid in schools. All of these involve an outside agency coming into the setting to train you to administer the correct first aid, as and when required.

In addition to first-aid courses, all staff within primary settings are required to attend sessions to raise awareness of ailments that are now commonplace in schools, including asthma training, diabetes training and allergy/EpiPen training, to name but a few. The training (which is provided by experienced medical practitioners) is very important, as it ensures all members of staff in school are aware of the signs and symptoms of these conditions and the procedures that should be followed if an emergency occurs within the setting (whether this be a child, member of staff, parent or visitor to the setting).

Tips

Tip 1: Have 'alert cards' up in the classroom. These should have a picture of the child on them, the triggers for an allergy and emergency numbers for anybody who needs to be contacted should the child be exposed to anything that may cause a reaction. This will ensure *everybody* who enters the classroom (whether cleaner or head teacher) knows which children may need emergency treatment.

Tip 2: In the setting I work in, we have a picture of a hand backed with red paper, with the class name clearly written on it. In an emergency, a child can take this 'red hand' to the office. Office staff call for an ambulance and a member of staff who is trained in first aid is immediately sent to the classroom. The 'red hand system' has two main benefits. Firstly, it saves the child from having to remember a long message and getting into a panic, and secondly, it means the adult does not have to leave the scene of the emergency. (The adult can remain there to provide reassurance to the child.)

Tip 3: Have a list of children who require asthma medication clearly visible in the classroom.

Tip 4: Make sure that the kitchen staff and dinner supervisors know which children have allergies, need inhalers or require medication. In some settings, coloured bands are now used at lunch times to indicate the child has an allergy; and for extra safety, a badge may be placed on the child before lunch, indicating what the allergy is.

Safeguarding (police officer/social worker/counsellor)

I have learnt over my time as a TA that in order for children to be able to learn effectively, they need to feel happy and safe. Therefore, part of your role is to be vigilant and raise any concerns you may have about an individual child or family, however small these may be. Before you even enter the classroom I would strongly recommend you read your setting's safeguarding policy, as it will clearly set out the procedures that need to be followed if any concerns about a child arise in the setting. (Although a lot of the information regarding safeguarding will be generic, certain information will be specific to the setting.)

There is now a requirement for all school staff to receive safeguarding refresher training every year. This is done to ensure all new and existing staff receive the most up-to-date safeguarding information. This training is essential, as it provides a comprehensive overview of the different types of safeguarding issues that can arise, and highlights any new issues that may arise during the current academic year, e.g. female genital mutilation (FGM) and the Prevent agenda (see p. 15). The training informs of the procedures that need to be followed when a concern is raised.

The term 'safeguarding' is used every day in educational settings. But you really do know what it means in practice. Safeguarding is: protecting children from harm (whether mental or physical); making sure children are being brought up in an environment that allows for their physical and emotional needs to be met; and ensuring that all children are given the opportunity to reach their full potential. As a TA, your role is teaching children how to keep themselves safe, recognising when they may be in danger and who they can ask for help. At times, you may become aware of an issue or concern regarding one of the children you work with, as a result of overhearing a conversation, watching the child interact with their parents, observing the child playing in the playground, seeing the behaviour of a child change over time, or from a disclosure made by the child.

Curriculum

Over the last few years the curriculum has changed dramatically and is now far more focused on highlighting the issues surrounding safeguarding and what children can do to keep themselves safe. PSHE (personal, social and health education) sessions, Dot Com and PATHS (promoting alternative thinking strategies) are just some of the strategies that have been introduced recently. All of these approaches provide children (either in small groups or in a whole class) with the opportunity to explore and discuss ways in which they can express themselves and keep themselves protected when in certain situations: e.g. being bullied, peer pressure, taking drugs, drinking alcohol, etc. By talking about these topics in a safe and controlled environment, children are able to identify the qualities needed to help them tackle or overcome these issues; the words 'supportive', 'trustworthy', 'strong-willed' and 'honest' recur during these sessions. Taking part in these lessons often has a positive effect on the children, as it gives them the chance to gain clarity on matters they may not be able to raise with adults, as the topic is seen as 'too embarrassing', or they are not sure of the correct way of asking. When answering questions, it is important to be as truthful as possible, within the remit of your role. See the tip underneath; this may help when answering a difficult question.

Tip

Tip 1: If a child asks a question and the answer either may not be entirely appropriate or may offend parents in some way, you might like to say: 'You may need to ask your parents that question when you get home' or 'I love that question. Maybe you could look it up on the computer when you get home.' Once you have said this, you need to speak to the parent and explain where the question came from. Often, once the parents know the context in which the question was raised, there is no problem.

Abuse

When a child enters the setting in the morning, it is impossible to know what they have experienced since leaving your care the previous day. It would be lovely to think that all children have an idyllic childhood, but, unfortunately, one thing this job has taught me is that we rarely have a true picture of the kind of life the children have outside of the setting. Over the years, I have learnt that there are no particular traits to families, no particular type of child that has an unhappy home life. You cannot always tell whether a child is going through a tough time at home. Any child within the setting could be seeing or experiencing domestic violence (DV), sexual abuse, verbal abuse or neglect on a regular or daily basis. Therefore, it is important to know what some of the signs of abuse are.

Signs of abuse

The thought of a child who is in your care suffering some kind of abuse is horrific. It is definitely the most daunting part of my job. But, as a professional, you always need to be aware of the signs and symptoms of abuse, no matter how small the signs are. Although training can provide you with a good understanding of the signs of abuse, sometimes you will just get a feeling. (Call it TA instinct, but you will 'just know' that something is not right.)

Common signs of abuse include:

- A sudden change in behaviour: a child being moody, withdrawn, clingy, anxious or having angry outbursts.
- Unexplained marks on the body, which may be seen when children attend swimming lessons or get changed for PE sessions, or the child not wanting to get changed in front of others for fear of someone seeing the marks, especially if they have been told not to show people.
- Coming into the setting looking unkempt, e.g. unwashed or hair and teeth not brushed, and wearing the same uniform for a number of days.
- Entering the setting looking tired and dishevelled.
- Eating food quickly, 'shovelling down food' or stealing food.
- High levels of unexplained absence from school (where the explanations given by child and parent vary dramatically).
- Talking about sexually explicit or inappropriate content of films and games.
- Always late in the morning/not wanting to go home at night.
- Often making negative comments about themselves/with low self-esteem.
- Finding it difficult to join in conversations about home life or family situations, e.g. birthday parties, visits and other family members.
- Can find the most basic tasks challenging due to a lack of concentration.
- Going on multiple extended holidays during term time.

The first time a child discloses information about any of these safeguarding issues can be a very distressing and extremely frightening time. But when this happens (and it will happen at some point in your career) you need to remember that you are there to listen to whatever the child has to say and get them the appropriate help and support needed as soon as possible. It is also important to note down what has been said to you as soon as you can. Any concerns of a safeguarding nature (no matter how small) must be reported to the designated safeguarding lead (DSL) immediately. This is normally the head teacher. However, if the DSL is unavailable or off site, then other members of the senior leadership team must be contacted, as they will also have received the designated safeguarding person (DSP) training.

Prevent duty

In response to recent events, all staff in schools are now required to receive training on how to support children who may be vulnerable to becoming radicalised to either support terrorism or take part in terrorist activities themselves. The Prevent training alerts staff to possible behaviours or signs vulnerable children may show in the setting, if they might be at risk of becoming radicalised. The possible signs can include:

- Children talking about terrorism in a positive way, or praising news stories where acts of terrorism have been reported.

- Radicalised views being aired during religious education (RE) lessons in response to opinions and beliefs offered by other children from other religions (which can sometimes lead to a child refusing to take part in RE sessions).

- Children talking about what parents have said in relation to news stories.

- Offering negative comments in response to other religions and beliefs and refusing to accept that other people are entitled to their opinions.

- Reeling off views and beliefs, as if the children have been programmed/'brainwashed' to say them.

- Talking about watching videos that have violent or inappropriate content.

- Poor attendance or persistent lateness, as children are taken to religious ceremonies when they should be attending school.

Sometimes, a child may do or say something that makes you feel uncomfortable, and you may have doubts about whether what you have seen or heard are signs of radicalisation at all. However, no matter how small the concern is, you must pass it on immediately to a member of the senior management team, in line with the setting's anti-radicalisation/Prevent policy. Remember to trust your gut instinct (it is normally right).

If no one from SMT is available, then it is possible to make a referral to the multi-agency safeguarding hub (MASH team) yourself. Normally, during Prevent training, the contact details for making a referral are provided to the staff. However, if this is not the case, then you can look up your local MASH team details online, so that if the need arises, you can report a concern about the safety and well-being of a child.

Tips

Tip 1: Read the setting's safeguarding policies and procedures and make sure they are kept close at hand.

Tip 2: Join a trade union as soon as you are working in your role as a TA. If you are ever accused of any wrongdoing by a child or parent, then the trade union will be there to support you; GMB and UNISON are just two of the unions that accept support staff as members.

Tip 3: If a disclosure is made to you, listen to the child and never judge them.

Tip 4: Never promise a child that you can keep what they have told you 'a secret'.

Tip 5: Never ask leading questions, for example: 'Did your dad give you those bruises?' or 'Did your mum hit you?'

Tip 6: Have a colleague with you when speaking to a child. This will enable detailed notes to be taken whilst you are listening to what the child is telling you.

Tip 7: Pass on the notes about concerns to the DSL in writing, as well as verbally. (The notes are often made after the initial disclosure has been made.) Both the TA and colleague present must sign the notes to say that they were both in attendance when they were being made.

Emotional difficulties

At times, children may come into the setting looking upset and distressed because of a problem they are experiencing outside the setting, e.g. parental separation or divorce, or bereavement of a friend or family member. These issues can have a negative impact on self-esteem and may also affect children's ability to concentrate in the classroom. But no matter what the problem, the child may need support to cope with whatever difficulties they are going through.

As a TA you are often the person who has the 'time' to take children out of the classroom to talk about any problems the children may be experiencing. Just letting the child know that you will listen to them if they need to talk is sometimes enough to help the child feel better. I have, on many occasions, seen a child look as though a weight has been lifted off their shoulders (this is sometimes called offloading) once they have talked about a concern or issues they might be having. However, it is important to remember that, as part of your duty of care, you must make a record of these 'talks', just in case a similar thing happens again, a pattern emerges or the situation escalates and becomes more serious than first thought. By noting down these concerns, you will have the times and dates of when the child was actually experiencing these difficulties, should any outside agencies require this information: e.g. social workers, key workers and/or the police.

Practical ideas

Have a book in the classroom where you log any concerns a child may be experiencing in school or at home.

Develop an emotions board where children can express how they are feeling, without the need to speak about it.

Ensure children have access to emotion cards, so that they can show you how they feel, if they are unable to name their emotions.

Tips

Tip 1: When talking to a child about a concern, *always* make sure you sit in a room where you can be clearly seen. A vulnerable child can sometimes make up stories, in order to gain attention.

Tip 2: Talk to your line manager about receiving training that will help you support children who may be experiencing social and emotional difficulties (this again will form part of your CPD).

During the last 17 years I have been given the opportunity to attend courses that have enabled me to support children through the most challenging of circumstances. Key courses have been:

- drawing and talking
- listening matters
- protective behaviour.

The first two courses teach strategies that encourage individual children who are experiencing difficulties to express their feelings through drawing and art. Drawing allows the child to open up and explore their problems without having to talk about them out loud. Sometimes, drawing the situation and talking about it in the third person can benefit the child immensely. You often find, the more a child draws, the more access you are given to their world (their subconscious): what is going on, who is involved and how they are feeling about the situation that is causing them to be anxious.

When I was first trained to use these strategies, I admit I was sceptical. I did not think that art and drawing would get me to talk to complete strangers about my inner fears and worries. However, during the first session, that is exactly what I did; I talked to complete strangers about issues that I had never talked to anyone about before. This experience taught me how valuable these art-based strategies are, and how important drawing can be when working with vulnerable children.

The protective behaviour strategy is based on a series of lessons based around the topic of personal safety and can be delivered to small groups or in a whole-class situation. It encourages children to identify: what is meant by the terms 'safe' and 'unsafe'; where their 'safe place' is; who makes them feel safe; and what in the setting or wider community may make them feel unsafe. By the end of the sessions, it is hoped that the children are able to identify a network of friends and family they can go to should they have a problem. As well as familiar people, the programme also encourages the children to think about which professionals could be contacted should an emergency arise, such as: police officers, social workers, counsellors and religious leaders, if appropriate.

Outside agencies

There are times when a child comes into the setting so distressed that far more support is required than you are trained to give. At this point, it may be necessary to pass your concerns onto the SENDCo, who can make a referral to an outside agency. Such agencies can offer far more specialised support to the child and the family in overcoming the difficulties they may be facing. The outside agencies that have been instrumental in supporting children in the setting where I work have included: a play therapist; school counsellor; educational psychologist (Ed Psych), child and adolescent mental health services (CAMHS) and Malachi (specialist family support services in Birmingham). But it is important to remember that during these times of austerity, the services offered to children may vary, not only between settings, but also between local authorities.

Tips

Tip 1: Parental permission must be sought before any interventions are carried out, whether for play therapies, counselling or observation by an outside agency.

Tip 2: Talk to the parent and involve them in the talking and sharing process. (Remember they are the experts on their child.)

Tip 3: Talk to the SENDCo, as they will be able to let you know about previous interventions already tried with the child.

Tip 4: Always ensure the child knows that sessions are confidential. But *make it clear* to the child that if any child protection issue (CP) arises, the concerns will be passed immediately to the DSP.

Educational visits (tour guide)

Educational visits are some of *the* most important events in the school calendar, as these not only help to pre-tutor children on up-and-coming topics, but can also reinforce what the children have been learning. They can also provide a 'WOW' moment to start a topic, which can inspire the children's learning. I love taking children from the setting, as this allows us to see them in a different context, and vice versa. It is also amazing to provide children with opportunities they may never have had before; even riding in the coach and seeing animals in the field for the first time can generate many questions. However, educational visits need to be considered carefully in these times of austerity. Visits I have been lucky enough to attend in my inner city setting have included: aquatic centres, farms, libraries, art galleries and activity centres; but there are endless possibilities.

Risk assessments

As the health and safety of all the children in the setting are paramount, teachers are now required to complete a risk assessment form, so that the head teacher can see what trip is being proposed; which activities the children are going to be taking part in; which members of staff are accompanying the children (so that staff:child ratio can be checked); what medical conditions the children have; what SEN the children have; what learning outcomes the visit will be targeting; and what preparation needs to be carried out before the visit takes place. It may also be necessary for you to take part in a pre-visit, which provides you with the opportunity to think about all the possible risks the children and staff could face during the visit. As a TA, you may be asked to go on the pre-visit as an extra pair of eyes, seeing dangers that may not be identified by other colleagues.

Some of the risks identified may be generic risks for all visits, e.g. trips, falls and illness. However, some risks may be present for specific trips or visits: e.g. bites from animals (if visiting a farm or zoo); interacting with members of the public (the cinema, aquatic centre, public library); and crossing roads.

It is important to remember that children can get themselves into troublesome situations when they explore areas in which they have never been before. Many a time, I have taken children from the setting to farms, and children have genuinely pointed at cows and not known what they were (there aren't many cows in inner-city Birmingham). Even where risk assessments have been carried out, there may still be times when accidents or unforeseen circumstances occur. So that you are prepared (if the unthinkable happens), I strongly suggest that you take the time to read the setting's educational visits policy and speak to the person who has organised the trip, to find out in addition what emergency procedures the relevant venue has.

Children and medication

Any time children are required to leave the premises, you will need to take their medication with you, whether for a bus/coach journey away or a visit around the local area. In the setting where I work, inhalers for asthmatic children in Year 6 are carried by the children themselves, whereas EpiPens (for those children who have allergies) are carried by the members of staff who are responsible for the group in which the child with the allergy has been placed. Any other medication is kept with the colleague who has the child in their activity group. In order to ensure the correct medication is taken on the visit, the medicine policy needs to be referred to, so that no oversights occur. However, it may also be necessary to check with colleagues to clarify what procedures the setting uses to ensure the appropriate medication has been packed for each child, so that if treatment is needed, it can be administered immediately. It is important to remember that some children may need medicine *before* going on the trip, e.g. motion sickness medication. In this situation, it is important to speak to the parents about when and how much medicine is required, and to check that the medicine provided has been prescribed by a doctor. (The chemist's label must clearly state the name of the child and the dosage that needs to be given.)

To make sure the relevant medication has been packed in preparation for the visit, the setting could use a medication checking form. An example of the form I use in my current setting is underneath:

Name of child	Class	Medical condition	Medication required	Packed	Medication packed by (staff name and sign)	Date	Seconded by (staff name and sign)

By having a checking system in place, a child will always have their medication when needed, and no child will be taken off school premises without the required medication.

Children with behavioural issues/medical problems

Taking children to a new place, especially those with medical and behavioural issues, can be an incredibly stressful experience. Therefore, it is important for the instructors/teachers to know what special needs the children may have before the visit takes place. This allows for strategies and advice to be given about how best to support the children in completing the activities, ensuring they get the most out of the visit.

By providing the information, the chances of children having an accident or being at risk will be significantly reduced.

Behavioural issues and medical problems that instructors need to be made aware of	
ADHD	Hearing impairment
ASD	Visual impairment
ODD	Asthma
Learning difficulties	Epilepsy
Cystic fibrosis	Spina bifida
Mobility issues	Diabetes

Tips

Tip 1: Send a consent/payment letter to parents well before the visit date, allowing plenty of time for payments to be made.

Tip 2: Prepare a class list and tick off when payments have been made and when consent forms have been returned.

Tip 3: Ensure every member of staff has a copy of the risk assessment, as it will have a list of their groups on it and emergency contacts.

Tip 4: Take a copy of the risk assessment with you to give to the instructors, so they are aware of things they might need to look out for.

E-safety (IT technician)

The skills children are now expected to learn through the IT curriculum are vast and really do reflect the importance of children becoming digitally literate. Computing (sometimes referred to as information technology (IT) or information communication technology (ICT)) is now an integral part of the curriculum and can, when used effectively, enhance the education the child receives. The use of applications/apps (whether this be on tablets, laptops, interactive whiteboards/IWBs or mobile phones) can provide children with a wealth of knowledge and experiences that are simply not possible without the Internet. Part of your role may be to support children during computing sessions; therefore you need to know about which systems staff are expected to use in the setting, the programs the children use and the different ways in which they can be used.

If you are anything like me and have a limited knowledge of IT, it may be necessary for the setting to arrange some training; such training will not only enhance your own skills but also provide you with the confidence needed to support children as required. Training will also provide you with information about E-safety (ensuring adults and children know the dangers of using digital and android devices as well as the Internet). To clarify your role when supporting children throughout an IT lesson, it is important to read the setting's E-safety policy, which will provide you with guidance on how to ensure all children stay safe, and how to report it if they are not.

Research

Using digital and android devices can provide children (and adults) with the opportunity to research topics that would be impossible to experience in person: e.g. World War 2, The Great Fire of London, Egyptians and Victorians, etc. However, using these devices comes with many dangers, which will need to be highlighted to the children, as part of the computing curriculum. Recently, it has become clear that some of the more popular search engines, such as Google and Bing, are not as child-friendly as first thought. On a few occasions, I have seen inappropriate content pop up for the children to view (even when the safety filters have been turned on). The role of the TA is to emphasise the need to use more appropriate search engines: e.g. Kiddle, Ask Kids, KidRex and Yahoo Kids.

Social media

Children at primary age (4–11 years) are now required to carry out basic coding, send and receive emails, post ideas on message boards and take part in chat room discussions ('chats'). In order to do this safely, settings can now subscribe to software applications (or apps) that will allow children to practise these skills in a way that can be closely monitored. *Moodle* is one such program, which I have seen used effectively in many settings; it provides children with the opportunity to use all of the skills covered in IT sessions, with the knowledge that their teacher will be there to support them should they need it. However, when using more widely used social media sites at home, such as Facebook, Instagram and Snapchat, the supervision may not be as stringent as it is in the setting. As part of the IT curriculum, the children need to learn about how to use the Internet safely. The E-safety message must be a key part of every computing session and be regularly repeated to parents whenever the opportunity arises, e.g. at parents' evenings and at Inspire workshops.

As the use of social media has grown, so have the dangers associated with it. Our setting, and other settings I have had the pleasure of visiting, use the SMART way of teaching children E-safety, to great effect:

S	Stay safe.
M	Don't meet up.
A	Accepting files can be dangerous.
R	Reliable?
T	Tell someone.

Alongside this strategy, you could also try using the following:

Tips

Tip 1: Ask parents and children to sign a home/school agreement, where both parties agree that digital devices, such as computers, mobile phones and tablets, will be used responsibly both at home and in the setting.

Tip 2: Organise E-safety workshops for parents. These will give parents the opportunity to experience the benefits of using technology for themselves and their child, but also help to highlight the possible dangers.

Tip 3: Have a book where you can record any concerns a child has about using specific devices or websites.

Tip 4: Keep up to date with the latest social media crazes, as these change often and can have a huge impact on the children in your class.

Practical ideas

Put words and phrases on the inside cover of laptops to remind children of the possible dangers they may face when using the Internet:

* Only go on websites you know you should be on.
* If you think something is wrong, then report it immediately.

During a computing lesson, you may want to help the teacher demonstrate the dangers of using the Internet by sending an email to the teacher, telling them they have won the lottery. Ask the children what they think about the email:

* Did they believe the email?
* Who sent it?
* How do they know?

It is a really good way of showing children that some people on the Internet are not who they say they are.

To explain how far-reaching social media is, you could post a picture on a social media site, asking people to share and comment on the picture. By carrying out this experiment, the children will be able to see how far a picture or message (they may have not meant to post) can reach, and what kind of damage it could do.

Tips

Tip 1: Be clear that it is illegal to set up a Facebook account if the child is under the age of 13.

Tip 2: Inform children of the dangers of posting pictures online, especially when wearing school uniform, as people may be able to track them, based on the school logo.

Tip 3: Make sure children do not give details about where and when they are going to meet a friend, as undesirable people can come and find them.

Tip 4: Advise the children never to meet people they have 'met' on the Internet, as these people may turn out to not be whom they were expecting.

Tip 5: Instruct children to tell an adult immediately if someone on the Internet asks them to do something that feels wrong or makes them feel uncomfortable.

Cyber-bullying

Over the last few years, in both local and national news, a growing number of issues around the use of social media and how this can be used to carry out 'cyber-bullying' have been highlighted. Some of these cases have led to devastating consequences, with children self-harming or committing suicide as a result of the bullying experienced.

As you know, young children now have unprecedented access to digital devices, often meaning that bullying can now happen anywhere. Cyber-bullying incidents can be really serious, as the child can feel as though nowhere is safe – not even in their own bedroom. It is important to remember children may feel at risk during computing sessions, out of fear that the bullies will somehow be able to contact them or get to them during these lessons. Part of your role will be to remain vigilant and listen to the children. As you work with the children, you may become aware of cases of cyber-bullying, either as a result of overhearing children speaking about an incident, or by another child approaching you with a concern. If you are alerted to an issue relating to cyber-bullying, it is important to report it immediately to a member of SMT, so the incident can be dealt with in accordance with the E-safety policy of the setting.

Once a concern has been raised, IT technicians or computing staff (who have the technical knowledge needed to advise on an appropriate course of action) will contact the parents of the child who has been experiencing the bullying to arrange a meeting. The meeting will provide the opportunity for the child to give their account of what has happened (times and dates), the content of messages (whether this be bad language, threats or nasty comments) or whether there was a reason the incidents started (as a result of an argument or disagreement). The meeting will also allow the setting to advise the parents and child on procedures that need to be followed in response to the incident.

A separate appointment will also be arranged, to talk to the parents and child who was responsible for the bullying, to inform them what has happened and alert them to the possible consequences of the child's actions (e.g. in-house exclusion or permanent exclusion, depending on the severity of the bullying). Often, the mention of these consequences is enough to stop the bullying. However, if the bullying continues, it may be necessary to request police involvement. This may result in more serious investigation and consequences.

Tips

Tip 1: Teach children how to save or screenshot messages, so they can be used as evidence, if need be.

Tip 2: Tell children safe ways to report cyber-bullying incidents. In our setting we have a system called 'Confide'. When the child logs on, the Confide logo pops up on the screen and if anything happens while they are on the computer that concerns them, the children can click on the icon and type in their concerns. The IT technician can then investigate these issues immediately. Also, many social media sites now have a button (CEOP button – Child Exploitation and Online Protection Centre) that can be pressed if the child feels uncomfortable with something they have seen or heard on the Internet. But, although many children know about the CEOP button, many children still fail to press it, out of fear they will somehow get into trouble for pressing it.

Tip 3: Teach children how to 'block' unwanted messages on android or digital devices and social media sites.

E-safety for adults

Whenever the term 'E-safety' is mentioned, we automatically assume it relates to the children. However, E-safety is not just for the children. Adults in the setting are also at risk of the dangers of the Internet. Settings are now required to provide annual E-safety training for their staff to remind them that the Internet could jeopardise not only their personal safety, but also their professional status. At a recent briefing, one of the most prominent dangers mentioned was from social media sites, specifically from using Facebook. The most important things to remember when using this site are:

• Under no circumstances accept a pupil who presently attends the setting as a 'friend' on any social media site.

- At no time accept past pupils as 'friends' on social media sites.
- Never add parents (whether past or present) as 'friends' on social media sites.
- Ensure privacy settings are set correctly (so only 'friends' can see the pictures you post). It could cause no end of upset if thoughts, views or photographs were seen or heard by people for whom they were not intended.

In addition to highlighting the dangers of social media, the training also points out the dangers of using school systems to carry out personal tasks, such as banking and emailing, as all passwords are saved automatically by the server. I know it is easy to consider doing these tasks during your break times or dinnertimes; but you must carefully consider who can access your personal information.

By completing the E-safety training, you, the TA, gain a good understanding of the dangers that the Internet can present to both children and adults. This enables you to explain these dangers when necessary, in a way that can clearly be understood by the parties concerned.

Interior designer (painter and decorator)

You may laugh, but throughout the setting there will be many display boards, each with a different purpose; some will be needed to celebrate children's work, to inform parents of up-and-coming events, and to display work about topics that have been covered by the children. But it will be your responsibility (under the direction of the class teacher) to decide how best to use these display boards to maximum effect. However, before putting up any displays, you should make sure you know exactly what is required from the display. I have heard of some settings that require the TA to double-back all display work, and to make sure the gap between each piece of work is the same and the work is placed the same distance from the edges of the display board. So, please ensure that you check the display policy in your school before a single staple gets fired from the gun tacker. It would be a great shame if all of your hard work went to waste.

Completing your very first board can be a daunting task, especially if you are not the artistic type (which I am definitely not). But there will be lots of people within your setting who will be creative and who will be more than willing to help you. You just need to ask.

Practical ideas

Talk to the other teachers and teaching assistants who work in the setting, as they will be able to tell you all of the dos and don'ts for displays.

Use dedicated display websites, such as:

https://www.superteacherworksheets.com/

http://www.instantdisplay.co.uk/

http://www.senteacher.org/

http://www.twinkl.co.uk/

All of these websites are full of practical ideas and unusual ways of displaying work the children have created. (Believe me, all of these sites are brilliant at saving you time.)

But don't be afraid to let your creative juices flow when putting up a display (it normally produces an eye-catching effect). Don't be afraid to ask for help when putting up your boards; backing paper can be tricky at the best of times and does not always cooperate.

Good work/celebration board

One of my favourite parts of the job is to show off the work the children have produced in response to a particular topic or event they have experienced, e.g. the rainforest, a trip to the farm or a visitor in school. The recognition the children receive can motivate and encourage them to work hard and try their best in all subject areas. A really good way to show the children you are proud of their work is to surround the board with positive words and phrases, e.g. 'proud', 'good', 'excellent', 'tried hard' and 'good effort'. You may also wish to add certificates to the board that have been awarded to children for the work.

To ensure the praise has maximum impact on the child's self-esteem, the certificates can be presented to the child in a class assembly, a phase assembly or in a 'celebration assembly', where the parents can be invited into school to watch their child be presented with the certificate.

Tips

Tip 1: Ensure the names of the children are written clearly on the certificates.

Tip 2: Make it clear why the child received the certificate. Be specific about which aspect of the work was good, and why it was chosen to receive special recognition, e.g. the child was able to demonstrate a good understanding of the use of punctuation; good presentation; correct spelling; good use of imagination and creativity, etc.

Parents' notice board

The parents' notice board is an extremely important part of school life, as it not only helps to keep them informed about any up-and-coming events, but also helps to make parents feel included in their child's education and part of the school community. The board can also act as a reminder to parents about when children need to bring things into school, e.g. snack money, PE kit, library book, revision books, trip money and consent letters, to name but a few. At different times throughout the year, the board may also be used to invite parents into school to participate in activities alongside their child. In the setting I work in, these sessions are called Inspire workshops. These workshops encourage parents to come into school and learn about the methods their children are now being taught in school (often very different to the way the children's parents were taught). This shared experience is invaluable, as it not only provides the parents with the skills needed to support their child at home with their studies; it also reinforces the importance of education and lifelong learning.

Practical ideas

Always keep spare letters on the notice board, so that parents can take another one if they have mislaid the original.

Make sure you keep a copy of all the letters that have been sent home to parents close at hand. I have had occasions when parents have told me that they have received letters about dinner money being made cheaper or snack money being reduced. If unsure, I have then gone back through the letters to check. When I have found the letter in question, it has said that for a themed dinner it costs £2.00 instead of the normal £2.15. Due to a misunderstanding, the parent has then started sending the lesser amount as payment for a normal dinner. But by showing the parent the letter, the confusion is soon cleared up.

Tips

Tip 1: Make sure all letters for parents are clearly marked with the date.

Tip 2: Have a timetable on the board so that parents can check when equipment is needed in school:

Monday	Snack money Dinner money PE kit
Tuesday	Painting apron
Wednesday	Packed lunch for trip
Thursday	
Friday	PE kit

English board

The English board can be an incredibly powerful tool that can be used to promote the good work that children have produced in response to work on a particular author, or some other topic covered in an English lesson. Celebrating the achievements made in English-based activities can have a massive impact on self-esteem and make the children more likely to take a risk; this can, in turn, develop their learning. However, to make sure that everyone gets the benefit of these effects, it is important to ensure the work displayed on the board truly reflects all the abilities within the class. In the setting where I currently work, all practitioners are encouraged to display the best piece of work from all children (whatever this may be); the work does not have to be spelt correctly or uniformly presented because this is simply unrealistic. However, I do know of other settings where displayed work has to be word-processed, spelt correctly and presented in a very prescriptive way.

Practical ideas

Provide children who find presenting work difficult with alternative ways of recording their ideas or findings. The use of either a laptop or a camera is a good way of encouraging children to participate in their learning; even the most reluctant child will embrace digital technology. This will ensure the focus is on the knowledge the child has of the topic, and not on their handwriting or presentation skills. Making this small change will have a huge impact on the child's self-esteem. It will make them not only feel that they can achieve academically, but also ensure that their opinions, thoughts and feelings are listened to and valued.

Maths board

Although maths is not a speciality of mine, I do recognise the importance of promoting the use of maths in everyday life; it can introduce new vocabulary and concepts and reinforce topics that have been previously taught to the children. The use of photographs can be enormously beneficial, as it can clearly show: the process the children went through to produce the work; what the activity was; which practical apparatus was used (Numicon, Base Ten and counters, to name a few); who the children worked with to complete the activity; and questions that were generated in response to the task. Through having created many boards, I have found out that the more interactive a board is, the more effective it is. A good way to achieve this is to add a variety of questions to the board, as well as competition entry sheets. By turning the content of the board into a competition, children in the setting will be encouraged to read what is on the board and go home and carry out research in order to find out the answers to the questions posed. The competition aspect will introduce children from other year groups to new topics and, of course, inspire independent learning, the need to take part and the desire to win.

Working walls

Over the last few years, settings have moved away from having many formal boards in classrooms and moved towards using working walls. Work carried out in the core subjects – English, maths and science – is modelled to the children by you and the teacher, e.g. how to write a sentence; how to improve the sentence; or how to complete a number sentence. The notes are then displayed in the classroom at child height, around the room. Children can then refer to these during the lesson, should they get confused, or simply forget what they need to do next in order to be successful.

Tips

Tip 1: Make sure the title on the display is bold and bright, so that everyone knows what the display is about.

Tip 2: Ensure the full names of the children are typed or written clearly on every piece of work displayed.

Tip 3: Use 'blurb' and photographs of the children completing the work. (This can then be kept as evidence for Ofsted.)

Tip 4: Make it clear what is good about the work, and why it has been chosen for display.

Tip 5: Make sure you refer to the information on the board regularly, as this will help to reinforce the child's vocabulary and understanding of topics covered.

Tip 6: Include work from *all* children in the class over the academic year, regardless of ability.

Tip 7: Ensure the board is as interactive as possible. This can be achieved by simply adding a whiteboard to the display, so both children and staff can write a response to any questions posed on the board, or give opinions about the work produced.

Rules board/class charter

Recently, the name of the rules has been changed in many schools in England in order to reflect the UNICEF Rights of the Child agenda, and they are now referred to as 'Classroom Charters'. The 'rules' agreed by staff and children have a massive impact on the success of the children, their learning and the setting as a whole. A good time to discuss these is at the start of the year, as one of your first tasks, as it helps to establish the boundaries from the outset, and sets the tone for the whole year. The charter can provide the opportunity for the teacher, TA and children to have a discussion about what is expected from them within the setting, whether this is in the classroom, when moving around school or in the playground, or when interacting with other children and adults within the setting. A good way to reinforce the importance of rules is to ask the children and all the other members of staff who come into that classroom (TA, learning mentor, dinner supervisor and SLT) to sign them, thus showing they agree to abide by them. This sends a clear message to the children that in order for there to be a calm and orderly school, the rules must be followed by everyone, staff and pupils alike. To reinforce the need for rules further, the charter must be placed in an accessible place, so both teacher and TA can refer to them if and when a gentle reminder may be needed.

Tips

Tip 1: Set the rules at the start of each academic year and keep on referring to them as and when needed. This clearly sets out the expectations of behaviour in and around the setting, and avoids any misunderstandings.

Tip 2: Put children's photographs around the edge of the rules board to show that all children are part of the class and can make a difference.

Tip 3: In the past, I have displayed expectations on jigsaw pieces, train carriages and hexagonal pieces (all with the children's names on). These all symbolise that the children are all part of something bigger and need to work together as a team, in order to make good progress.

There may be occasions where children in the setting are not allowed to have their pictures taken, for whatever reason. If this is the case, offer an alternative. Ask the child to draw a picture of something that represents them or their hobbies, e.g. football trophy, doll, etc. This will ensure the child still feels like part of the class.

Goals board

I love putting up the goals board, as it gives children something to aim for during the time they are in your class. At the very start of the year it can serve as a really nice 'getting to know you' activity; and it can also help to gauge the attitude to learning of both the children and their families. However, it is important that the board be revisited at the end of the academic year as well, as it sends out a very clear message to the children. It shows them that they can achieve something, and that every improvement (no matter how small) is noticed and valued. By celebrating these achievements, the children will not be afraid to wish positive things for themselves in the future.

Tips

Tip 1: Make sure the goals set are written by the children in their own words. There is no point in making up the goals for the children, no matter how well intentioned.

Tip 2: Place words and phrases around the board that truly reflect and celebrate differences. These may relate, for instance, to children's religions, languages, culture, home life, likes and dislikes, etc.

Tip 3: Put up pictures that challenge stereotypes (e.g. female firefighters, male nurses) as this will help to support some of the long-term goals set by children, regardless of their gender.

You have now come to the end of the first chapter. I do hope you have found it useful and that I have managed to provide you with some helpful ideas, tips and time-saving advice that you may use in the future. But I also hope that I have not scared you into thinking about joining another profession. I have tried to be as honest as I can when telling you about some of the tasks a TA is expected to carry out during an average day. I am not going to lie; the job does get tough at times, and certainly tests your time-management skills and patience to the absolute limit. But I hope the message that has come through loud and clear is what a massive impact you, the TA, can have upon children, whether it be on their academic ability, their confidence or their readiness to learn while they are in the setting. It is truly wonderful to look back at the end of the year and see the extent of progress the children have made. It makes all of the hard work well and truly worth it.

Chapter 2
Supporting children with special educational needs

This chapter aims to provide you with a brief overview of the special educational needs and disabilities (SEND) that you may encounter in your role as a TA and advice on how best to support the children with them. Children with SEND often have some difficulty when trying to access the curriculum or participate in their learning. The degree of support the child may need in order to access the curriculum can vary massively, from you working alongside these children within the classroom, to working in small intervention groups, or on a one-to-one basis, to help them overcome these difficulties. It may seem overwhelming at first, but the more experience you gain, the easier it will get. One thing that will stand you in good stead when working with children with SEND is to read the SEND policy from the setting and read up on the types of difficulties children may experience whilst in the setting.

However, to write about all of the special educational needs and disabilities (SEND) you may encounter within a mainstream primary school would be impossible. Therefore, I intend to provide you with a brief overview of some of the more common disabilities, conditions and learning difficulties that you may come across in a mainstream primary setting. These are (the umbrella term) autism (which now covers autism, autistic spectrum disorder (ASD) and Asperger's syndrome); attention deficit hyperactivity disorder (ADHD); dyslexia; dyscalculia; dyspraxia; oppositional defiant disorder (ODD); obsessive compulsive disorder (OCD); hearing impairments (HI) and visual impairments (VI).

One of the most rewarding parts of the job is to see the improvements children with SEND make throughout the year (just you wait and see). Knowing that you played a part in that progress is difficult to put into words – just magical. Once you have done the job for a couple of months, you will look back at all of the work the child has done with you, and I guarantee you will see a difference, no matter how small.

Oppositional defiant disorder (ODD)

When I first started in my role as a TA, I had never heard of oppositional defiant disorder, as there were no children in my setting with a diagnosis of ODD. However, over the last few years there have been more children who have been diagnosed with this condition. As with any SEND, the behaviours displayed vary from child to child, but from experience, children with a diagnosis of ODD can often get frustrated in a classroom setting very quickly, especially when being asked to follow an instruction or complete a task they do not want to carry out. This can often result in the child becoming argumentative with whichever adult has given the instruction, whether this be the teacher or TA. If things do reach this stage, you need to know that this can often escalate very quickly into physical aggression. Therefore, you need to sit down with colleagues and devise ways of trying to minimise the stress felt by the child in the setting:

- Build up a good relationship with the child that has ODD. This will help the child feel happier in the setting and make them more likely to comply with what is being asked of them.

- Talk to the child about the kind of words they would like you to use when directing them to do something.

- Ask the child what triggers their feelings of anger, and what you can do to help them feel calm again. If the child does not know what the triggers are, it may be necessary to speak to the parents, as they will have calming strategies they may wish to share with you.

- Put a visual timetable up in the classroom, and another one on the child's desk, so that the child knows exactly what to expect on a day-to-day basis.

- Ask the setting about the possibility of restraint training. This will provide you with calming strategies and safe handling strategies if and when you should need them.

Another part of the school day that can be problematic for children with ODD is playtimes and break times, as the child can often become involved in arguments or altercations with other children. It is not that the child intentionally goes out to have a fight or argue, but part of their condition is to point out what other children are doing 'wrong' and want the unacceptable behaviour dealt with by a member of staff immediately. However, the other part of the condition is the inability to accept responsibility for anything they have done wrong. At times this can be incredibly frustrating, but you must tell the child why their behaviour may have caused the situation to escalate, as well as deal with unacceptable behaviour identified by the child with ODD.

Practical ideas

Provide the child with a quiet area that they can access at playtime, break times and other times of stress. *Make sure the area is staffed by somebody who has a good relationship with the child (if possible a named person or key worker).

In the setting where I work, the quiet area is supervised by a learning mentor (LM) who has a range of activities on offer for the child or children to participate in.

Having to conform to the rules of school, all day, every day, can be incredibly difficult for a child with ODD; so it is important to build 'time-out' sessions into the timetable. Having time away from the stresses of the classroom can help to keep the child calm and ready to learn when they re-enter the classroom. Ten minutes of physical activity (running and playing football are particularly good) can often help the child get rid of any pent-up anger. As you gain experience and begin to build up a relationship with the child, you will know which strategies will help to keep the child calm, and which will not. Once this is in place, the child will not only be able to participate in their own learning, but will also be able to access the curriculum.

Activity	Benefits to the child
Using Nintendo DS™	This encourages the children to make positive relationships with people they would not normally play with (especially if they can choose a friend to play a Nintendo DS™ game with as well).
Using e-readers	Reading something the child enjoys often calms a child down, as they will frequently become so engrossed in the book that all of their anger disappears.
Colouring in (of pictures that interest the child: cars, fairies and trains)	Colouring in is legendary for its calming effect (not just for children – I have often found myself colouring in right next to the child).
Craft activities (painting, home-made play dough and decoupage)	Craft of any description requires the child to concentrate on the art, rather than the issue that made them angry in the first place.

However, there will be times when you have used all of the approaches that normally help to keep the child calm, and they have simply not worked. It happens to everyone, even the most experienced TA. Do not despair; dealing with these behaviours every day can be extremely stressful and difficult to deal with, but it is important to remember that you do not have to deal with it on your own. In every primary setting, there is a whole team of professionals to support you: the class teacher, the SENDCo and the behaviour coordinator (BECo) to name but a few. *All you have to do is ask!* I know asking for help is often seen as a sign of weakness, but it is not. We have all been there – believe me!

Obsessive compulsive disorder (OCD)

OCD is increasingly being diagnosed in primary-aged children. The needs of any one child with OCD will be particular to that child alone and can vary immensely from child to child. Some children will need to have set routines; some will require all of the classroom equipment to be labelled and organised properly; some children may need to check or recheck tasks that have been completed to make sure they are satisfied with the outcome; some may need to wash their hands and keep their clothes, desk and area around them tidy. This need for tidiness may result in the child finding it difficult to participate in any activity where they could get dirty. All of these difficulties can be overcome if you work alongside the teacher, child and parents to think up some ingenious ways to carry out practical activities that will help alleviate some of the stresses brought on by the child's condition. Here are a number of things you could try:

Tips

Tip 1: Always have a visual timetable up, so that the class knows what to expect during the day (lessons, trips, visitors and any changes to the day). You could also have a smaller copy of the timetable attached to the child's table, so that they can refer to it throughout the day.

Tip 2: Make sure all of the classroom equipment is clearly labelled with words (and pictures if needed).

Tip 3: Encourage all of the children to put equipment back where it belongs.

Tip 4: Have a pack of hand wipes available for the child to use if and when needed.

Tip 5: Set up a range of alternative activities that can be used by the child if they start feeling distressed or uncomfortable during the lesson.

It is important to remember when a child tells you that they need to carry out a task in a certain way that the child has no control over it; they really do need to complete it in that way. If the child is stopped from completing the task in the way they need to, it can cause an enormous amount of stress. Although this can be incredibly frustrating for you, it is important to listen to the child. It will soon become apparent to the child that you care about them and that you are prepared to go out of your way to help them overcome their difficulties. By building up this trust between you and the child, the child may try new things (as they will have you there to support them).

Practical ideas

Talk to the child about which parts of the school day they find difficult: the classroom, the lessons (whether this be the pace or content), break times or dinnertimes.

Give the child the option of setting up the equipment themselves, so that they have control about where the equipment is going to be placed.

Provide the children with different (more OCD-friendly) activities that enable the child to meet the same learning objective (LO). *Instead of finger painting, the child could use stones, leaves or other objects to paint with.

Attention deficit hyperactivity disorder (ADHD)

Children with ADHD can often find school a traumatic place, as the expectation of them to complete work and conform to the rules of the setting is often too much for them to cope with. If this is the case, children can often become frustrated, angry or quiet and withdrawn in the classroom. Children with this condition can also find it extremely difficult to engage in their education as their attention span, as the name suggests, can be very short. This can make concentrating long enough to complete a task problematic. At times the child may also be impulsive, which can result in the child shouting out answers and not giving the other children the opportunity to participate in the lesson. But if the child has a dedicated person (such as a TA) who is prepared to use a variety of strategies to develop the child's ability to concentrate, take turns and engage in tasks for longer periods of time, then progress will be made. The progress may be slow and the amount of strategies used can seem monumental at times, but perseverance can bring great results.

Practical ideas

To help overcome the impulsive shouting out, a tub of lollipop sticks can be amazing (believe me, I know how mad this sounds). Each child in the class or group has a lollipop stick with their name on it. If you or the teacher require the children to answer a question, you ask the child to pick out a lollipop stick. If their name is written on the stick, they can give the answer to the question asked. If it is another child's name, then that child gets to answer the question. Giving them this job will hopefully alleviate the need to shout out, as they will be far more excited to see whether their name is written on the stick, or whether they need to wait for another turn.

Set up a friendship group with children who are good at modelling turn-taking, as this can be incredibly effective with children who have ADHD. In these sessions the children can learn turn-taking skills in an informal, friendly and non-threatening way by playing games, such as Snap, Ludo and Happy Families. These types of games will encourage the child to wait to take their turn, negotiate with their peers and practise their conversational skills.

Have a box of activities that the child can access if they start to feel stressed:

- Colouring sheets are very effective, especially if the picture is of something the child has a real interest in; cars, trains and fairies are some of the most popular colouring-in sheets I have used over the years.

- Maths puzzles can be used quite effectively when a child is feeling uneasy, as the child has to concentrate on the task in hand, rather than whatever it is that they were angry about.

- Squidgy toys (or a little blob of Blu-Tack™) are good, as they give the child a way to vent their pent-up anger.

Tips

Tip 1: Keep instructions to a minimum and use language that is clear, precise and to the point.

Tip 2: Break the task up into small, manageable pieces. Depending on the child, one instruction at a time may be all they can manage.

Tip 3: Build rest breaks into the timetable, so that the child knows how long they need to concentrate for.

Tip 4: Use a variety of stimuli to engage the child in their learning: sport, computers, cars and any other interests the child may have. Weaving these into the curriculum will encourage the child to become involved in their learning.

Once you have been working with the child for a while, you will get to know what triggers the child to shout out, what stresses them out, and when things simply get too much for them. At this point, it would be a good idea for all of the professionals involved with the child to discuss how best to meet the needs of the child and design a handling plan. Of course, the main aim of the plan must be to keep the stress the child feels within the setting to a minimum. It will also ensure all members of staff who come into contact with the child react to their behaviours consistently. The child will then need to be taken somewhere quiet and talked through the plan, so that they are aware of which member of staff will be working with them, what they are required to do in the allocated time, and where they are going to be taken to complete these tasks or activities. If on the plan it says that you should work with the child at a set time, then you must try your best to be there. If you are unable to be with the child due to unforeseen circumstances (as can happen in a primary setting) then explain to the child why you could not be there, and arrange another time to work with them. Being honest and truthful with the child can help develop trust, which can, in turn, help the child make real progress in the setting.

However, sometimes things do not go to plan, and it may be necessary to remove the child from the classroom to either stop the behaviour escalating further or to stop the education of the other children being disrupted. Of course, before removal is considered, you will make use of all the calming strategies and distraction tactics you know. But, if these tactics do not work (and sometimes they don't), you may have to seek assistance from other members of staff in the setting: the SENDCo, the class teacher or the learning mentor. If the behaviour of the child escalates further, and they are at risk of hurting themselves or others, you may need to contact members of SMT. This may result in the parents being phoned to either come into school to try to alleviate the situation or, as a last resort, to remove the child from the classroom and take them home. If the behaviour continues once the child returns to the setting, external agencies may be required to come in to advise staff on how best to meet the needs of the child. Some strategies that have been tried and tested include:

Tips

Tip 1: Make leaving the classroom 'informal' by providing the child with a 'time out' pass, so that the child can remove themselves from situations that are causing them to become distressed.

Tip 2: Give the child a timer, so that if they do need to leave the classroom for any reason, they know when to return to class (the amount of time needs to be negotiated).

Tip 3: Provide the child with a 'leave lesson early' pass, so that the child does not have to walk down a crowded corridor with the other children.

Tip 4: Allocate the child with a key worker or named person (this *does not* have to be you) to talk to about problems or difficulties they may be experiencing in the setting.

Tip 5: Offer the child a quiet and safe place to go if they need time out of the class. Some schools are lucky enough to have a sensory room, but in others it may just be a quiet room, library or an unused classroom.

Tip 6: Know where the restraint forms are, so that you can fill in the necessary paperwork (if it has been necessary to physically remove a child from the classroom to stop them hurting themselves or others). *Remember to do this as soon as the incident has been dealt with.

When supporting a child with ADHD, it is important to remember that the strategies that have worked well for one child with the condition may not work for another child with the same diagnosis. All children are different and have different triggers, interests and coping mechanisms, and can react differently, depending on the situation they find themselves in.

Autism

Working with children who have autism is my absolute passion (although I do have a vested interest – my son Jack is 13 years of age and has autism). I hope this part of the chapter will provide you with lots of practical ideas and strategies you can use when you have a child with autism in your class (and you will definitely have a child or children in your class with autism). During my time as a TA, I have heard many terms used to describe a child with a diagnosis of autism; these include: autism, Kanner's, Asperger's syndrome and autistic spectrum disorder (ASD). All of these terms now come under the umbrella term of autism. Autism is a developmental disorder for which there is no cure, and is a lifelong condition. I have learnt from reading various books, attending many courses on autism, and through working with children with autism, that there are all kinds of theories and thoughts about possible causes and traits of autism. But what has become clear is that there are some common features or 'traits' to people on the spectrum; these are often referred to as the 'triad of impairment'. The term, as the name suggests, refers to three clear areas that all children with autism have some degree of difficulty with: social interaction, language and communication skills, and a lack of imagination. However, after attending some autism-awareness training recently, I have also become aware of a fourth area that can affect a person with autism: sensory issues.

As soon as you find out you are going to be supporting a child with autism, I would suggest you complete these four tasks as a matter of urgency. Firstly, spend some time in the classroom working alongside the teacher in June/July, so the child gets to know you before they enter their new classroom in September. Secondly, produce a transition booklet that contains pictures of the new teacher, the TA (I know you are groaning at the thought of having your photograph taken) and other key members of staff (head teacher, deputy head teacher and office staff who will greet the child as they enter school). As well as people who work in the setting, the transition booklet may have pictures of key areas of the school the child will visit regularly: classroom, toilets, canteen and playground. Thirdly, complete a pupil profile, which will provide you with the opportunity to find out information that could help if the child gets upset or worried about anything. The final task I would suggest you do with the child is complete an environmental checklist. The checklist will help you to identify which areas of the setting a child has difficulty with.

Putting in this extra effort before the child enters the classroom will pay off in the end, as it will alleviate some of the stress the child will be feeling about all of the changes a new academic year brings: classroom, teachers, teaching assistant, routines and ways of working. It will also give you the opportunity to think about how the learning environment is organised to best meet the needs of the child. By working alongside the child and parents, with the support of the teacher and SENDCo, it may be possible to make the smallest of changes to the classroom, playground, dinner hall or any areas that cause distress. If this is done effectively, it can not only have a positive impact on the child at the very beginning of the academic year, but can also impact on the child's self-esteem and their ability to participate in their learning in the future.

Funny story

A while ago I found out I was going to be supporting a child with autism (at the start of the next academic year) so I started to prepare a transition book with my photograph in it. However, over the six-week holiday, I had my hair cut and had it dyed my natural colour (instead of the grey that had started to show through). When the child walked into the classroom he looked at me and said: 'Miss, I like your new head. Did you get it over the six weeks' holidays?'

Making sure you are knowledgeable about autism is key to the progress the child will make in your classroom, so reading as much as possible about autism is essential. It will help you develop an understanding of the common difficulties a child with autism may experience within the setting, and which strategies can be used to support the child through difficulties.

The difficulties a child with autism can face on a day-to-day basis can vary massively, depending on the setting, the situation they find themselves in and the environment. The classroom, playground, dining hall, and being taught by certain members of staff can all be common causes of anxiety and distress. If the child's anxiety levels continue to rise, then it can result in the child getting into such a state they lose the ability to listen to instructions, and all logic disappears (you will often hear colleagues referring to this as a 'meltdown'). Your role at this point is not to reason with them, but just be there to listen to them and make sure the child does not hurt themselves. Witnessing a meltdown for the first time can be a bit overwhelming and can often be misunderstood by other staff and interpreted as the child being naughty, rude and, at times, stubborn. However, once you get to know the child, you will quickly learn which behaviours are traits of their autism and which actions are used as delay strategies by the child, to avoid a task they find difficult or simply do not want to complete. If you are not sure whether the behaviours are down to the diagnosis of autism, talking to the parents would be my first port of call. Parents can often shed some light on the actions of their child (sometimes something has happened at home in the morning that makes the child anxious, and this continues to affect them all day).

Practical ideas

Invite the parents into the setting before the child joins the class, as the transition from class to class can often be a very frightening and stressful time for both the child and parents.

Spend time with the child before they join your class, so the child can get used to your ways of working and the expectations of behaviour and level of work you have.

Have a copy of the SEND policy at hand, just in case you need to refer to it to check about strategies that can be used to support a child with autism.

As part of your CPD it may be possible to ask for the setting to send you on an autism course, to provide you with a basic knowledge of the condition.

Social interaction

In order for anyone to interact successfully, there are a number of skills that need to be mastered. Most children with autism have some degree of difficulty with social interaction. The common problems include:

- Taking turns in a conversation (listen and then wait for a response).
- Responding to the other person appropriately (both verbally or through facial expressions and body language).
- Giving and maintaining eye contact.
- Showing active listening – by nodding and making noises that show they are listening to what is being said.
- Approaching an adult in the setting to ask for help (whether this be the teacher, you the TA, supply teacher or a dinner supervisor).

To most children the ability to interact with their peers comes naturally. However, children with autism often find these skills difficult. Children on the spectrum are unlikely to approach others in order to initiate a conversation; this can result in the child coming across as unfriendly and cold. As a result, the child may be labelled as odd and often end up being left on their own. But children (even those with autism) can be taught to become competent in the art of social interaction and this is where you with your expertise come in. There are many different activities and strategies that can be implemented to encourage the child to try out interactions with other children and adults, in a range of 'safe' situations, with you there for support and guidance:

Tips

Tip 1: Send the child with a friend to give a message to another member of staff (pre-warn the other teacher that the child will be coming, so they give the correct response).

Tip 2: Set up social interaction groups (SIG) so that the child can practise turn-taking and the negotiation skills sometimes needed in order for a successful conversation to take place.

Tip 3: Organise friendship groups, with children who are proficient in conversation, so that the child can practise talking in a fun and informal way (often through the use of games).

Tip 4: Use mirrors to encourage eye contact (with themselves first) and then small amounts of eye contact with a friend they feel comfortable with.

Children with autism often have difficulty understanding the rules of communication, e.g. talking and then waiting to listen to the response, using and reading facial expressions and gestures, reacting appropriately to a difficult or awkward situation they may find themselves in. Often children with autism will say exactly what they think and feel and have no thoughts about how this may upset or offend the person they are saying it to. This, as you can imagine, may result in the child finding it difficult to make and maintain friendships, as the child is often perceived as 'odd' or 'eccentric'. Another common difficulty that a child with autism has is the giving of eye contact. Some children I have worked with over the years have described how giving eye contact makes them feel physical pain. Therefore, children with autism should not be forced to maintain eye contact. However, it is possible to teach the child to look at a specific point on a person's face, to show they are in fact listening to what is being said.

Practical ideas

Produce a pupil profile for each child with a diagnosis, to ensure that all staff in the setting understand what makes the child with autism feel uncomfortable when asked to give eye contact. The last thing we want is for the child to get into trouble unnecessarily.

Understanding emotions is difficult at the best of times; but a child on the spectrum is often not able to interpret facial expressions and body language. This can often result in the child not being able to use them appropriately either. At times this can result in a child having issues with other children in the setting, as they have responded to an issue in a way that they have felt was appropriate, but other children not. If this keeps on being repeated, the child may find it difficult to be accepted by the other children and start to feel isolated. However, throughout the day there will be many opportunities for you to model appropriate facial expressions and label feelings. Make sure you are really explicit when naming an emotion to a child with autism. If you feel happy, make sure you smile. Alternatively, if you feel upset or sad about the behaviour the child has shown, then show them a facial expression that reflects your feeling. If your facial expressions do not match what you are telling the child, the child could feel like they are being given conflicting messages and feel anxious and worried as a result.

Physical contact is another area where a child with autism can struggle. Over the years I have found that when it comes to physical contact, children on the spectrum can go one of two ways. Either the child is resistant to any kind of physical contact, or they love hugging and touching other children. But what often causes problems is the child's lack of understanding of what is appropriate and what is not. As part of your role, you may need to teach children what physical contact is appropriate and what is not acceptable. Common issues I have had to deal with in the past have included:

- The child hugging other children in the playground either too tightly or refusing to let go, even when they have been asked to by the other child (you may think this is lovely – but not when you have to deal with the fall-out every break time).

- The child punching another child, and when asked why they have done this, telling you it was only a joke.

Tips

Tip 1: Play games based around facial expressions and body language. Children could pick up a card with a facial expression on it. The child has to name the emotion. When the child gets more confident with naming the emotions, the child can pick up an emotions card and act out the emotion to a partner or small group. This encourages the child to practise naming their emotions in a safe, supportive environment.

Tip 2: Set up a SIG, using other children as good role models for communication. However, you must be careful that these children do not take over the group, as this can have a negative effect on the self-esteem of the child you are supposed to be helping.

Tip 3: Show children how to play games to practise turn-taking, asking questions and negotiating. These are skills that are needed if the child is to become proficient in the art of communication. Snap, Happy Families, Monopoly® and draughts are just some of the games that I have found to be effective.

Tip 4: Model appropriate touch to the child (either individually or as part of a small group) and give the child the opportunity to practise these skills. A good way to do this is to use toy figures, as they give the child the opportunity to show what physical contact would be appropriate if they were feeling angry, happy, upset or excited.

Language and communication skills

As with all aspects of any disability, the level of difficulty can vary from child to child, and language and communications skills are no different. Some children in the setting may be able to verbalise their ideas, thoughts and feelings about a particular topic. However, there will be children in the setting who will be non-verbal. Although this can be difficult, part of your role will be to invent and use a variety of strategies that will enable the child to take a full and active part in their learning (don't worry, there are plenty of tried-and-tested ideas below).

Within the curriculum there are many words, phrases and concepts that can be extremely confusing to a child on the spectrum, as many ideas are based on abstract ideas (things the child cannot see and touch). PSHE is one such subject – e.g. what is 'society'? A child cannot see 'society'; they cannot touch society and manipulate it. Therefore, it is part of your role, alongside that of the teacher, to look at the child as an individual and think about how best to teach them these difficult topics. Although it is important to expose the child to all areas of the curriculum, it is also vital that both the explanations and work are at the right level for the child, so the child feels as though they are able to achieve in each subject.

It is important to remember that whilst some children with autism are able to talk, some are not able to talk at all (non-verbal), while others just lack the confidence to verbalise their thoughts and ideas to people they are not familiar with. At times, this can be incredibly frustrating as children often need to ask a question or make a request and they are simply not able to do so. However, whatever the situation, I am sure you will be sensitive to any attempts to communicate and think of some imaginative ways to support the child with their difficulties.

Tips

Tip 1: Use signs and symbols so the children can use the symbols to: ask to leave the classroom if needed; communicate thoughts and feelings; write sentences; and respond to what they have been asked (for this, the Widget program is highly recommended).

Tip 2: Provide the child with a laptop, tablet or computer, so they can communicate with you through typing instead of speaking.

Tip 3: Providing the child with a picture stimulus that the child can point to will give you some idea about what the child has understood, or what they may need more support with. *Smiley and sad faces are sometimes helpful for the child to say how they feel about a particular topic or situation.

Tip 4: Depending on the level of understanding the child has, it may be beneficial to attend either a British Sign Language (BSL) or Makaton course. Talk to your line manager and ask about the possibility of training.

Tip 5: Talk to the Communication and Autism team (CAT team), who will be able to provide you with lots of practical activities and advise on how to support children with autism.

Practical ideas

Speak to the IT department (or if you don't have an IT department you can contact the IT coordinator) about which programs or apps could be used to support children who have communication difficulties.

Contact the SENDCo to ask how the use of IT can benefit children with a communication difficulty.

Once you start working with children who have autism you will quickly realise that another common difficulty they tend to have is organising their thoughts and ideas to complete tasks: e.g. collecting the right equipment for a lesson, putting their clothes on in the right order and completing work in the correct order. However, there are many things that you can try, to make life a little bit easier for you and the child.

Tips

Tip 1: Place visual instructions or sequence cards on the desk in front of the child, to encourage the child to become independent and self-check which tasks have been completed so far, and which still need to be finished.

Tip 2: Break the task into small, manageable pieces, so the amount of work does not overwhelm the child. A sand timer is sometimes a good way of ensuring the child focuses on a task for a small amount of time.

Tip 3: Get the child to repeat the task back to you after the teacher has set it; this will let you know whether the child has understood what is being asked of them. But remember, just because the child has nodded or told you they have understood, this does not necessarily mean that they have.

Practical ideas

Write the name of the child on all of their equipment (pen, pencil, crayons, ruler, eraser and calculator) and place it on a basket on their table, so that the child does not have to spend valuable learning time worrying about where their equipment is. This will also help alleviate some of the stress the child may feel before being asked to complete a task.

In addition to having difficulty organising equipment, thoughts and ideas, a child on the spectrum can find it hard to respond to instructions, as they are often unsure of what is expected of them and how the instruction applies to them. When giving the child an instruction, you must make sure you get the child's attention by saying the child's name at the start of the instruction. Once you have got their attention, you can then go on to give them an instruction. Just because the child has listened to the instruction does not mean they have understood what is being asked of them. A good way to check their understanding is to ask the child to repeat back the instructions they were given. However, you should never assume that the child understands the instruction just because they are able to repeat it back to you and nod furiously. During the lesson it may be necessary for you to go back to the child many times to check their understanding, break the instructions down into even more manageable steps and model the language that may need to be used in future tasks.

If the child follows the instructions straight away, it is important that you recognise this and give them praise immediately. By getting positive feedback, the child is far more likely to repeat this behaviour when asked to do something again. In the setting where I work, we have a saying: 'first work, then reward'. The rewards we use in the setting are decided through discussions with the children (with lots of adult guidance obviously!) so that the teaching and support staff can use these as an incentive for good work and for using appropriate behaviour in and around the setting. However, when setting the rewards, you will need to think about how you are going to manage them in terms of time and resources, as tasks like these often become part of your role as a TA. The rewards that tend to be popular in primary settings include extra playtime, time on the computer and a game of football.

Tips

Tip 1: Before giving an instruction always get the child's attention by calling their name and make sure they look in your general direction. Although most children on the spectrum have difficulty giving full eye contact, the child can be taught to look at a specific point on a person's face, giving the impression they are paying attention. By doing this the child will not only know the instruction is relevant to them, but also know that they will need to listen carefully to the whole instruction.

Tip 2: Once you have given the child an instruction, give the child some time to process what has been said. The courses I have attended have suggested that a child with autism needs six seconds more than a child without a diagnosis to process information.

Tip 3: Be prepared to repeat the instructions in a different way if needed (by using a picture stimulus or practical apparatus: e.g. Numicon, counters or sequencing cards). Showing the children how to complete a task using practical apparatus will help support and develop their understanding of a particular topic.

Tip 4: Give the child clear, manageable instructions. If you want to check the child has heard all of the instructions you have given, you can ask the child to repeat them back to you.

It is important to remember that children on the spectrum will take things very literally. When, on occasion, I have asked a child to 'wait there for a second', I have turned around and found them standing right behind me. When I have asked the child why they have not moved, they have said, 'Well, you told me to stand there for a second, and I didn't know what to do after that.' It is sometimes difficult to remember to use short, clear and precise language, especially when you are inexperienced. But, the more time you spend with the child, the more you will get to know about what the child understands and which vocabulary they struggle with. One way to stop any misunderstandings occurring is to avoid using sarcasm and metaphors when teaching. Such language can often cause an enormous amount of confusion for the child, as they will often take what is being said literally:

'It's raining cats and dogs outside.'

'Have you seen the smoke coming off _____ pencil today? He is working so hard.'

'You're on fire today – well done!'

'You really do need to pull your socks up.'

These are some of the most common sayings I have heard in settings over the years. I have quite literally seen children rush to windows looking for cats and dogs, jump up and drop pencils thinking they are on fire and look down and check whether their socks really do need pulling up. *This may sound funny, but the child can worry about the meaning of these saying for days, without telling anyone.

Funny story

I was once called into my son's primary school by a very angry teacher, who informed me that Jack (who has autism) had refused to get up from his table at the end of the day to get his coat and bag from his peg. The teacher told me that she had asked him to get ready several times and that each time he had ignored her. I asked her how she had asked him to do this. She told me that she had told 'red table' to get their coats and bags ready. I then asked Jack why he had not got up to get his coat and bag. He told me quite emphatically that his name was not 'red table'; his name was Jack. The teacher never called him 'red table' again.

Social imagination

One of the other traits of autism is the lack of imagination and rigidity of thought. Children on the spectrum need to have order, routine and consistency, and can get extremely anxious if things change. Therefore, keeping to a routine where possible must be at the forefront of your mind when planning activities and setting up classroom rules and routines. As we all know, primary settings are busy places where unforeseen circumstances sometimes crop up: a child is ill in the classroom, so the class have to move to another room; the teacher has to leave the classroom to deal with an issue; or OFSTED (Office for Standards in Education, Children's Services and Skills) inspectors turn up. If any of these happen (and they will) you must make sure you talk to the children as soon as possible, carefully explaining why things have had to change and what will happen next. However, if you become aware of changes to the school day in the near future, such as a school trip or a visitor coming into school, then you must tell the child in advance and keep on telling them as the event gets closer (a drip-drip effect). It may prompt the child to ask about the proposed changes to the routine over and over again, but in my experience this is only done so that the child can make sense of the new routine and understand what these changes will mean for them.

The way a child with autism can react to a change of routine can vary immensely from child to child. Some children can become angry and aggressive; others can become quiet and withdrawn; and a few can simply refuse to do what has been asked of them. As the change gets closer, you may notice an increase in unusual or unacceptable behaviours. It may be necessary to speak to the child again to go through what the change may mean for them. Do not be upset if the child does not listen the first time you try to discuss change; they are processing the change. As you get to know the child, you will be able to gauge the best way to tell the child about possible changes, in a way that keeps stress to a minimum.

Tips

Tip 1: Provide a visual timetable for the child that clearly sets out what lessons are going to be taught that day.

Tip 2: Have a question mark as one of the symbols on the visual timetable. The question mark will alert the child to the fact that something in their routine may change or may not happen the way they expect (e.g. the PE lesson may not go ahead because of bad weather).

Tip 3: Some children may not be able to cope knowing what is going on throughout a whole day. It may be necessary to break the day up into smaller, more manageable chunks of time; therefore, you may want to use a 'then, now and next' chart. For older children, it can give them the opportunity to reflect on the lesson or activity they have done previously, to think about what went well and what may need to be changed next time. However, for younger children, you may just want to use 'now and next', as they may find it difficult to remember what they did earlier in the day.

Then	Now	Next

Tip 4: Try to avoid putting timings onto the timetable (especially for the beginning and endings of lessons), as some children on the spectrum will spend the whole lesson clock-watching instead of learning.

Tip 5: Never use vague terms like 'maybe', 'later' and 'possibly', as the child may think that they have a chance of doing whatever they have asked about.

Practical ideas

Have a blank timetable on the child's desk for the child to make notes on. The child can record the good and bad points of the lessons, which lessons they feel confident in, and which lessons they are finding challenging. Using this strategy may help you to identify a pattern in the child's behaviour throughout the day – e.g. the child may start to feel ill before every maths lesson, or refuse to enter the classroom before a maths lesson is due to start. This could indicate the child is experiencing some kind of difficulty within a particular lesson and can provide you with an opportunity to talk to the child about their experience of the previous lesson and how the child feels about up-and-coming lessons. It may also help you decide upon things that can be done to overcome these difficulties or worries.

Obsessions (or 'passions', as they are now called)

Children with autism can sometimes have a passion for a particular object: e.g. an umbrella, dustpan and brush, vacuum cleaner, closing doors, light switches, to name but a few. But it does not have to be an object; over the years I have seen children be passionate about a wide variety of topics. The most common passions I have encountered over the last 17 years include: dinosaurs, cars, trains, football and characters from films, cartoons and programmes such as *Postman Pat, Star Wars, Bob the Builder* and *Thomas the Tank Engine*. When I first became a TA (a very long time ago) children with autism, who talked about their favourite topic all the time or carried around their preferred object with them everywhere, were said to have an obsession. However, this word has since been replaced with the word 'passion', as having an obsession with something was thought to have negative connotations.

When my son was diagnosed with autism at the age of five, he told the doctor he loved *Thomas the Tank Engine*. Now, at the age of 13, his passion is football (well, Birmingham City Football Club – I don't know if that's the same thing!). Jack has an amazing memory for facts and figures to do with football: e.g. goal scorers, times the goals were scored and the number of goals scored by players. Although I listen intently to what he is saying, I have never really understood why he loves football so much. However, now I have worked with many children with autism, I understand the second passion he has: Peppa Pig. It is all to do with the fact that all of the episodes contain some common features: all the characters appear in every episode; Peppa and George do activities with their friends; and life is generally fun, as the characters spend most of their time jumping in muddy puddles. In each episode there are no surprises, and Jack knows exactly what is coming up in each programme. George still makes him laugh, as does Daddy Pig's snort (even though he has watched the same episodes hundreds of times). Now that Jack is in a secondary setting, he is aware that some of his peers have an issue with him liking something that is 'babyish'. Even the football has caused problems. This is not because the children do not like football, but because Jack sometimes talks *at* his friends about football, instead of *to* them, and he does not listen to their responses.

A child who has a passion about a particular topic can often be seen as odd, and may be ridiculed by the other children. If this happens, it may be necessary for you to monitor how the other children react to this passion and set up interventions that may help support the child through the difficult time.

Tips

Tip 1: Set up a friendship group with children who have different interests to the child. This will encourage the child to listen to what other children are interested in, within a safe and supportive environment.

Tip 2: Give the child a scrapbook (with a picture of their passion on the front), which can be used by the child as a reward for working hard, making the right choice or following instructions.

Tip 3: Set up an after-school club to encourage the child to find out about or use their topic of interest. Chess, football or reading clubs can support children with autism.

Tip 4: Organise a coffee morning for parents of children who have a diagnosis, as this gives the parents a supportive environment in which to discuss any common issues and talk about possible solutions to any problems identified.

Tip 5: Offer a club to families who have a child with autism, where children and parents can meet together and share ideas and strategies that have been used successfully at home.

Tip 6: Use the strategies from the social and emotional aspects of learning approach (SEAL), if your setting uses this programme.

Tip 7: Allow time during the day for the child to talk about their passion. It does not have to take up lots of time; just a few minutes is all the children will need.

Encouraging the passion a child has and getting a real feel for what the child is interested in can be extremely important in the setting, as it can be used both to inform the planning and as a cross-curricular tool. This knowledge can not only motivate the child to be involved in their learning, but also motivate them to want to carry out independent learning. (Maybe the child will carry out research on a topic at home, or be inspired to talk to the rest of the class about what they have found out.) Underneath is an example of how a passion (in this case, football) can be used to motivate a reluctant learner:

Cross-curricular links (Football)				
Literacy/ English	**Numeracy/ Maths**	**Guided reading**	**History**	**Geography**
Newspaper reports	Statistics	Match reports	Match reports	Atlas work to find out where teams are situated
Writing a commentary for a match	Probability	Football magazines	Radio reports	National teams flags
Cartoons/ play scripts	Addition and subtraction	Comic strips	Statistics	World Cup activities
Role play/ drama			Team history research	

Sensory issues

All of us experience sensory overload on occasion: a light flickering, the noise of a lorry, or the sound of drilling outside the classroom. However, we have the ability to block out this distraction. Children with autism tend not to have this ability, which can cause the child to lose concentration, refuse to take part in lessons, or even refuse to enter the classroom at all. What upsets a child on one particular day may not affect them again the next day; the degree of sensitivity (whether over-sensitivity or under-sensitivity) depends on the situation the child is in and how they are feeling. So, when the classroom is being set up at the beginning of the academic year, it is necessary to think about the needs of the child and how the classroom environment could affect children with autism.

The classroom can often be full of distractions, which can make it difficult for the child to maintain their concentration and can cause them to experience sensory overload. Part of your role, alongside the teacher, is to try to keep these distractions in the classroom to a minimum.

During my time as a TA, I have seen many items in classroom environments that have needed to be changed or replaced, so that the stress felt by a child is kept to a minimum. I know that the TA's time is precious, but it is important to take the child out of the classroom and into a quiet area and ask them what aspects of the setting they find difficult and what causes them to become anxious. Listen to how they feel about the classroom and what is making them feel like this. It may also be necessary to invite the parents into the setting, so that you can find out what makes the child feel anxious at home and what strategies the parents use to calm the child down. Although all of this may sound time-consuming, it is important to find out what under-stimulates or over-stimulates the child's senses – it could be something they touch, smell, taste or hear – and make the necessary changes as soon as possible.

Sound

As I have said many times throughout this book, children with autism can react very differently, depending on the situation they are in. The range and levels of noise can cause a huge problem for some children with autism. This is because they can be incredibly sensitive to sounds and can react very differently to the many different sounds they hear on a day-to-day basis. Often, you may see the child cover their ears if a loud noise occurs: the door banging, the IWB buzzing, the teacher shouting or the fire alarm going off. In order to drown out the noise, you may hear the child making a louder noise, to block out the sound that is troubling them. At other times of the day, the same child may be tapping and banging loudly whilst they are completing their work (and will be totally oblivious to the other children getting annoyed), whereas at other times, the child may get distressed by the smallest noise e.g. another child tapping, chewing food or messing with VELCRO® shoe straps.

When the child is feeling upset because of a noise they have heard, there is no point trying to talk to the child or give them instructions, as they will simply not be able to listen properly. When a child has reached this point, it may be necessary for you to gently lead them out of the classroom into a quiet place, where the child can calm down and de-stress.

As well as noise levels in the setting, a child with autism can also become overwhelmed by the amount of instructions being given to them. This, again, may result in the child putting their hands over their ears and making a noise to block out what you are saying to them. Although this can be perceived as rude, the child is doing what they need to do to feel comfortable and this behaviour is part of their condition. In the setting where I work, every child with autism has a pupil profile card displayed in the classroom. The profile tells every adult who comes into the classroom about the child and their typical behaviours; this protects the child from getting into trouble for behaviour they simply cannot control.

Child Profile	
Name of child (and preferred name if different from the name on the register) with accompanying photograph	Diagnosis (with details of behaviours the child may show when distressed)
Likes: (these can be things the child does at home or at school)	Parent contact details (if a child has a meltdown or issue, the parent may need to be contacted as a matter of urgency)
Dislikes: (these can again be activities the child does at home or in school)	You can help me by:
Things I would like you to know about me:	Other strategies that help me to cope:
Things that I find difficult:	People who can help me:

Practical ideas

Invite the parents in to ask them about strategies they use to calm the child at home.

Have a 'noise-o-meter' on the child's desk, so the child can let you know what the noise level is like for them.

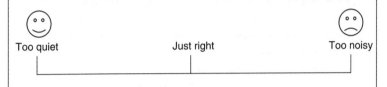

Too quiet   Just right   Too noisy

Tips

Tip 1: Use a neutral tone of voice when teaching and try not to shout (I know this will be difficult at times). By remaining calm, the child is more likely to listen and respond to what is being asked of them.

Tip 2: Give the child a set of ear defenders to use if the noise in the classroom disturbs them too much (although the child must take them off to listen to instructions).

Tip 3: Provide the child with a screen to put around their table, so that the working area is blank. To motivate the child further, you could add pictures to the inside of the screen of things they are interested in (passions).

Colour

In addition to sound, some children with autism can be sensitive to colours used in and around the classroom, which can cause them to feel anxious and even disorientated. The reaction to a particular colour may be so extreme that the child may simply refuse to enter the classroom at all. Part of the role of the TA is to talk to the child about which colours make them feel worried and which colours they feel happy with. Although any colour can be a source of distress to an autistic child, during my time as a TA, I have found that red and yellow are the two colours that most commonly cause problems to children on the spectrum. Once you know which colour is causing distress, the situation can be quickly and relatively easily addressed.

Other things in the classroom that may need to be changed are strip lighting and computer screens, as these are the two things that often cause problems when they flicker. These problems can be solved relatively easily: new tubes can be added to the lighting and screen filters can be added to the computer to minimise flickering. It may sound silly to change the lighting and screens all because of one child, but, believe me, these small changes can make such a difference to the child. The child will be able to focus on their work instead of the distraction.

Tips

Tip 1: Talk to the child about the colours that make them feel anxious; then make the necessary changes, if possible.

Tip 2: Ask parents about which colours can trigger the child's anxiety and which colours could be used in the setting to help make the child feel calm and relaxed.

Tip 3: Use neutral colours on display boards in the setting (I know using neutral colours goes against all of your natural TA instincts, but it really can make a massive difference).

Tip 4: Try not to have objects and information hanging from the ceiling, as these can sometimes catch the light and cause the child to become distressed and disorientated.

Funny story

I was working in a reception class at Christmas time. It was time to put the decorations up, so I asked the children to help me. One of the boys with autism ran straight up and shouted, 'Can I put the broccoli up?' I did not understand what he meant, and this puzzled the teacher and me all day. When his mum came to pick him up we mentioned it to her and she started laughing. She told us that he could not say the word sparkly so he said broccoli instead. She told me that he called tinsel sparkly. He had wanted to help me put the tinsel up. Of course, the next day I gave him the job of putting the tinsel (or sparkly) on the Christmas tree. Now, every year when I decorate the tree, I always put sparkly on the tree.

Touch

At times, everyone can feel the need to avoid being touched, and children who have autism are no different. In a classroom or setting where there are lots of people moving around, you will often notice some children looking incredibly nervous at the very thought of being touched, whether by a person or a certain texture. Although it is impossible to stop the child touching or being touched in the setting, it is part of your role to observe the child and talk to them to find out which parts of the day and which lessons cause the most stress. You may see a child become visibly tense when you are about to place a reassuring hand on their arm, or if someone brushes past them in the corridor. Children may also become stressed before taking part in activities that require them to touch certain textures. Over time, I have seen children get upset when introduced to sand play, painting and cooking activities for the first time. If a child gets themselves into a state, it may be necessary to work alongside the child to show them that they have nothing to fear. Older children may, point blank, refuse to take part in a task they feel uncomfortable with. But don't worry – you will use all of your TA skills to think of different ways of carrying out the activity. Remember what I have told you many times before: if you are struggling to think of ideas, then talk to other colleagues; they will be able to give you other ways in which you can support the child.

Tips

Tip 1: Carry out an environmental checklist, which will quickly identify any changes that may need to be made to make the classroom more accessible for children with autism.

Tip 2: Make the changes to the classroom environment as soon as possible, to keep the stress felt by the child to a minimum.

Tip 3: Allow the child to use tweezers or prongs or to wear gloves if you want them to try and use something with an unfamiliar texture, e.g. cloth, paint or wet sand.

Tip 4: Provide the child with a toilet pass, so the child can use the toilets at a time when they are not being used by lots of other children.

Tip 5: Give the child a 'five-minute pass', which allows the child to leave a lesson early (to go to the canteen or hall, or to run an errand) when the corridors are emptier than normal. *Hopefully, this will alleviate the chance of the child getting knocked or bumped on the way to their destination.

Smell

There will be times when a child gets very upset in the setting, but it will not be immediately obvious what the issue is. Observing the child may be the only way you will find out what is causing them to feel distressed. Part of the role of a TA is to make a record of when and where the child is, when the signs of distress occur (times, dates and places will need to be noted down). By doing this, you will be able to build up a clear picture of what is causing the problem. Sometimes the issue can be something that requires you to make a small change to the classroom or routine. However, more often than not, the issue is far more difficult to deal with (e.g. smells coming from the kitchen and the smell in the canteen at dinnertime) and can require the setting to think of ways to help the child overcome this.

Practical ideas

Go down to the canteen to collect the child's dinner, so the child does not have the stress of walking into the canteen (which is often too loud and full of food smells).

Talk to the child and ask them whether eating their dinner in a classroom or separate room would help them feel more comfortable.

Set up a 'buddy system', where sensible children in the class can be chosen to support the child with autism (don't worry; you can vet them before they are asked). Choosing 'popular' children to buddy children with autism can make the child feel accepted by the rest of the class.

Make sure the child can choose a friend or 'buddy' to eat with; otherwise the child may become isolated from their class.

Ask other members of staff to eat their lunch in the staffroom, rather than in the classroom, as smells from food can often linger and can make the child with autism feel physically sick, giving the child a negative start to their afternoon.

When talking about a child with autism, you will often hear colleagues talk about the child being hyper-sensitive or hypo-sensitive to something. If a child is described as being *hyper*-sensitive, the child on first glance can appear to be clumsy, regularly falling over, bumping into things and dropping equipment. This can have a massive impact on the child and their self-esteem. Children will often feel that they cannot take part in any physical activity (especially PE) through fear of failure. Therefore, it may be necessary to think of different ways to bolster the child's confidence, by showing the class the things the child excels at: e.g. working with a partner to catch (using a bigger ball) or playing rounders (by using a stand where the child can hit the ball from the top, rather than using their hand–eye coordination). These small changes will make a considerable difference to the child, and will give them the confidence to try something new.

Children who have this issue also tend to have a problem gauging where they are in relation to others (they are either too close or too far away). You will sometimes notice that this can cause a problem with their peers, as they often end up invading someone else's personal space. In order to overcome these issues, it may be necessary for the child to sit on a chair with their legs tucked underneath them, as they simply cannot feel the chair below them. On other occasions, especially just before a PE session, you may need to ask the children whether they are wearing pants or socks. Some children may need to look down to check, as again they will not be able to feel whether they are wearing them or not. This may be referred to as the child having difficulties with their proprioception.

Tips for children who are hyper-sensitive

Tip 1: Set up a gross motor skills group to encourage children to practise using their limbs to make controlled movements, such as kicking a ball, jumping with their legs together, walking in a straight line and moving in different directions to avoid objects. (See Chapter 5 for further ideas).

Tip 2: Organise a fine motor group, which will give the child the opportunity to improve their hand–eye coordination, which they need to complete tasks such as cutting with scissors, letter formation and writing. A fine motor group will allow the child the chance to practise their pencil grip. Sometimes children may press down on the pencil too much and rip the paper, while others may not press down on the pencil enough, making their writing incredibly difficult to read.

However, other children on the spectrum may be described as *hypo-sensitive*. You will be able to recognise these children instantly, as they will be the children who constantly:

- Jump around everywhere.
- Stamp their feet when they are walking around the setting.
- Play rough and tumble games, such as wrestling, where their friends have to hug and hold on to them as tightly as possible. (However, this also applies to lots of the boys in a primary setting.)
- Deliberately bump into people and objects; walls and doors are just some of the things the child may walk into on purpose.
- Spin around until they fall over.
- Wear clothes that are too tight for them.

Tips for children who are hypo-sensitive

Tip 1: Arrange a time in the day when it is okay for the child to bang and make noise; drumming lessons and music sessions are a good way to facilitate this.

Tip 2: Give the child a weighted blanket to place on their lap when they need to sit still, e.g. on the carpet for registration and in assemblies. The weight of the blanket gives the child the sensory feedback they require.

Tip 3: Provide the child with a 'bear hug' – a vest with VELCRO® straps that can be loosened or tightened, depending on the needs of the child.

Tip 4: Speak to the occupational therapist, who will be able to provide you with some practical ideas and activities that can be used to improve the child's gross and fine motor movements.

All of the traits (things that are common to people with autism) I have written about can make it incredibly difficult for a child to concentrate on their learning. The smallest thing in the classroom environment can easily overwhelm a child with autism. But it is important to remember that no children on the spectrum are the same; their triggers will be different, as will the things that calm them. Although this part of the chapter has focused on children with a diagnosis of autism, I hope that you will use some of these ideas with all of the children in your setting, as they will help to develop the language and communication skills needed for them to be able to access the curriculum effectively.

Dyspraxia

The number of children in the setting who are now being given a diagnosis of dyspraxia has steadily risen over the last few years. In each class I would say there is at least one child with a diagnosis of dyspraxia and at least one more child who is yet to be diagnosed. As with all of the other special needs I have written about, the problems a child with dyspraxia can experience vary from child to child, and depend on the situation the child is in. Some children with dyspraxia can often come into the setting with quite complex needs, which are obvious from the outset; others will need to be observed. (This is where your expertise comes in again.) Children can often come into the setting with fine motor or gross motor difficulties. Children with gross motor problems can sometimes have difficulty with walking on uneven surfaces, gauging their distance from other children (spatial awareness) and changing direction to avoid objects. The children with fine motor difficulties can have problems completing tasks that require them to use small movements with their fingers: writing, picking up small objects or tying shoelaces.

PE sessions, playtimes and times when children are moving around the classroom are all times that may help you determine the level of support the child will need. If you have completed an observation and are still concerned, then you and the teacher need to speak to the SENDCo (who is always my first port of call). The SENDCo will be able to tell you what can and has been done previously to help the child improve their gross and fine motor skills. This conversation may result in you being asked to set up a small intervention group to build on the support already given. However, if some of the needs are more complex, external agencies may be invited into the setting. These agencies will be able to offer you and other colleagues specialised advice and strategies that can be used to best meet the needs of the child.

Occupational therapists are just one example of the external agencies who could come in and make an initial assessment of the child and their needs. Once this has been done, they will be able to offer the setting some advice on ways to support the child to overcome their difficulties or develop strategies that will allow the child to cope with their condition. Children with dyspraxia may also benefit from seeing a physiotherapist. The physiotherapist can also come into the setting to assess the needs of the child. They can offer advice on what kinds of activities the child may need to carry out in order for the child to develop their independence. Offering training to TAs is sometimes appropriate, as the child may respond well to your instructions (as you will have built up a positive relationship with the child), which will enable you to make sure they are using the right techniques when doing their exercises regularly.

If you get to a point where you are running out of ideas or feeling unsure, remember there will always be colleagues in the setting who will have experience of working with a child with dyspraxia. It is always a good idea to speak to them and pick their brains about activities they have used before to improve either fine or gross skills.

Tips

Tip 1: Set up a gross motor skills group to give the child the opportunity to practise kicking a ball, walking on different surfaces, balancing, walking and jumping in different directions, and throwing and catching.

Tip 2: Organise a fine motor skills group that is going to allow the child a chance to practise their pencil grip, their pincer movements, and picking up and manipulating small objects (counters, buttons and money).

Tip 3: Get children to carry out tasks against the clock and against each other; the competition always helps the child to focus that little bit more.

Tip 4: Drop things on the floor from time to time, giving the child the opportunity to pick them up. Really praise the child when they are successful. By doing this, the child will become more confident in their abilities.

Tip 5: Use pegs to put up work on the walls and encourage the child with fine motor difficulties to help you.

Tip 6: Give the children patterns to trace over. These patterns are the precursor for letter formation. Tracing repeated patterns will help the child develop the movements needed to form each letter correctly.

Hearing impairment (HI)

There are, on occasion, children in the setting who have a hearing impairment, and, depending on the severity of the hearing impairment, will depend on help from specialist resources or equipment. Some children may need hearing equipment in the classroom or portable equipment that the child will need to take to activities that are not taking place in the classroom, e.g. a PE lesson, a school trip or assembly, to name but a few. If this is necessary, then the child will be regularly visited by the Hearing Impairment Team, who will check that the child is able to access the lessons, that the equipment is being used properly and that the child does not need anything else to support their learning. This team will again be able to provide help, support and advice on the types of resources and activities that can support the child at school and at home.

Practical ideas

Make sure the child with an HI sits near the front of the classroom, so that they can hear you more clearly or lip-read, if they have learnt this skill.

Ask the child to pick a talk partner (somebody they feel comfortable with, if they need to ask to clarify any misconceptions).

Keep a packet of spare hearing aid batteries somewhere handy, just in case they run out (it always seems to happen in the middle of a test or lesson).

Over the years I have worked with children with a variety of hearing aids: headband hearing aids, behind-the-ear (BTE) hearing aids and in-the-ear (ITE) hearing aids. These have all resulted in me using a variety of different devices to help the child access the curriculum; I have had to wear a 'smiley mic' around my neck, so the child could hear everything that was being said.

Funny stories

The first week I was given a 'smiley mic', another TA colleague and I found it difficult to remember to turn off the microphone when the lesson had finished. In one lesson my colleague suddenly said that her contact lens had slipped and that she needed to go to the bathroom. She left the lesson. When she came back, the child with the HI was laughing. The colleague asked the child why they were laughing. He said that he had heard her 'chuntering' as she was messing about with her contact lens AND he had heard her going to the toilet. She had forgotten to turn the microphone off.

On another occasion, another colleague had left the room, accidentally taking the microphone with her. At a crucial time in the lesson the child with the HI stood and hugged me. I said, 'thank you' and carried on teaching. A minute or two later the child stood up and shouted, 'Hello everyone!' I then realised that the other TA had been giving the child instructions through the microphone that she had taken into the other room.

Visual impairment (VI)

Children can enter the setting with varying degrees of sight; some children will come into the setting with very limited vision, while others will have difficulty seeing certain things in different lights or from a distance. Whatever the level of sight, the setting will need to decide what support the child will need so that they are able to participate in school life. If the child has limited sight, there are lots of adaptations that can be made to the setting to enable the child to get around safely. The changes I have seen in my time as a TA include:

- High visibility tape being placed on steps, so the child can clearly see where the stairs are.

- Signs around the setting can be enlarged, so that the child can get around the setting independently.

- Children being given access to the lift (if applicable) so that they do not have to use the stairs when they are crowded in with other children.

However, if the child has reduced vision, it may be necessary to make small changes to the classroom and resources to enable the child to access the curriculum. This could be as simple as: photocopying the text to enlarge the print; using different-coloured backgrounds on the IWB to make text stand out; or providing the child with thicker line guides and giving the child a laptop, so that the font and screen can be enlarged and personalised to meet the child's needs. However, some resources cannot be made and may need to be purchased by the setting. These can be found in special needs brochures, although you may have to grovel to the resource manager:

- Enlarged key word/phonics posters may be needed to ensure the child with VI can access them to the same degree as a child without a visual impairment.

- A 100 square or multiplication square that has been enlarged allows the child with the VI to see it from a distance.

- A magnifying glass is a brilliant way to promote independence; the child can decide if and when they need to use it.

- 'Big books' are a good way to encourage reluctant readers to share books with their friends.

- The child I currently support has a small monitor in front of him, which is linked to the main IWB. This allows the child to see the same as the rest of the class.

Last year, I worked with a child to support her with her VI; her teacher and I thought of many different ways in which we could help her access the curriculum. She had reached the time in her schooling where she was making the transition from a primary to a secondary setting. To help support her through this time, teachers from the Visual Impairment Team came to show the child how to make her way around the local area and practise taking the route to her new school. The same provision is going to be made for the child I am supporting this year, giving the child adequate time to get used to crossing busy roads, using a crossing and avoiding any possible dangers that may arise.

Tips

Tip 1: Talk to the children regularly to make sure that their needs have not changed.

Tip 2: Invite the parents to come in, to discuss whether the child may need their provision changing or whether it meets their needs.

Tip 3: Get a child to pick a friend to help them access resources from around the classroom.

Tip 4: Ask the child to pick a friend to help or escort them around the setting.

Tip 5: Produce the timetable in black/white and colour and talk to the child about which one they prefer.

Tip 6: Keep in regular contact with the SENDCo so that they are aware of any changes that need to be made to the provision.

Tip 7: Ensure that key words used on display boards are large enough for the child with VI to access independently within their work, especially when completing topic work.

Tip 8: Make sure the classroom is kept tidy and clutter-free (chairs tucked in) and children sit with their hands in their laps when sitting on the carpet. This will minimise the risk of the children falling or injuring themselves in the classroom.

Dyslexia

Although I have supported a few children over the years with dyslexia or where dyslexic tendencies have been identified, I have become aware of certain characteristics that may indicate a difficulty. The first one everyone thinks of is the child doing their b's and d's backwards. Although this can be a cause for concern, there are also many other characteristics that will surprise you, as they did me (when I was given a list by the SENDCo during a twilight session recently). Here are just some of the difficulties a child can experience:

- Often complains the text that is being read is moving or jumping around on the page, so finds it difficult to read at a fluent pace (which is needed to be able to gain a good understanding of what has been read).

- Spells the same word many different ways in the same piece of work.

- Gets frustrated and uses avoidance tactics if they are asked to write anything down (whether this be *informal* thoughts and ideas or *formal* writing to complete work).

- Has poor handwriting, as the child finds it difficult to form and join letters, as they simply cannot see how to do this properly, no matter how many times you have shown them.

- Struggles to follow a set of instructions. Although the child may follow the instructions, they might not be able to follow them in the right order.

- Gets mixed up between the left- and right-hand side of their body.

- Finds it incredibly difficult to copy down accurately from the board (often missing out letters or copying them down in the wrong order).

- May give the most fantastic answers orally, but finds writing their answers down very difficult (and what has been written does not resemble what they have said at all).

As I have said before, many times during the book, a child with a SEND issue can experience just some of these characteristics or all of them, as no two children are the same. What will work with one child simply may not with another, even if they have the same diagnoses. Do not despair, however; after speaking to other colleagues, there are many ways in which you can support children with dyslexia. I hope at least some of these may help.

Tips

Tip 1: Make sure the child is given lined paper to write on, which is not white in colour (this limits the movement of the words when reading and writing). It may also be necessary to give the child an overlay (of coloured acetate). It does not have to be expensive; coloured plastic wallets are effective, if they make it easier for the child to read and write.

Tip 2: Produce a word bank of 'common words' the child may need to use in their writing; this will stop the child becoming anxious or worried about not knowing how to spell a word.

Tip 3: Give the child a spellchecker, which only needs the child to type in the rough spelling of a word they are trying to use (and the checker will provide the child with the correct spelling).

Tip 4: Use the IWB as much as possible to play games and give the child the opportunity to play around with letters and words; Wordshark and Clicker are programs that I have used in the past, as have other colleagues I have spoken to.

Tip 5: Have time set aside during the day, or lesson, so the child can listen to storybooks, either as e-books from the computer or on a CD player. If the child can be given the book that goes with the story being read, the child will be able to point out repeated words and phrases. When the child grows more confident they may even start to read along with the story.

Tip 6: Talk to the child about what they find difficult and come up with a solution with the child; they will then be more confident when using any strategies you put into place.

Practical ideas

Talk to parents, to see if dyslexia runs in the family (as it often does). This will give you the opportunity to ask about any difficulties the child has at home and what strategies are used to support the child.

Use lots of praise and encouragement, especially when a child has attempted to read or answer a question in a small group situation.

Talk to the children regularly to find out what is working for them in the setting and what they are still struggling with; this will give you the opportunity to find out whether any other interventions need to be offered or whether the current provision is working well.

If you try these ideas and there is no improvement in the situation, it may be necessary to speak to the SENDCo, who may be able to offer more strategies that could be used to support the child further. However, if all avenues have been exhausted, it may be necessary to request a referral to an outside agency. With learning needs such as this, a referral tends to be made to Pupil Support Services (PSS). As with other SEND issues, the process starts when a specialist practitioner comes into the setting to carry out an assessment on the child.

Once this has been completed, they will produce an individualised programme of work and activities that will help the child to develop their reading and writing skills; this can be used by the teacher or TA to engage and support the child with their learning. The activities are often so much fun, the children do not even realise they are doing work.

Dyscalculia

As with many of the difficulties I have mentioned in this chapter, the number of children now being identified as having dyscalculia is steadily rising. Although I have worked alongside many children who enter the setting with a natural ability for maths, counting, identifying number patterns and making links between mathematical words and symbols, I have also supported a number of children who struggle to grasp even the most basic number concepts, even though none of them have ever been diagnosed with dyscalculia.

As you get to know the children, you will soon get to know when they are genuinely finding things difficult and when they are trying to delay working (we all do it). Some common difficulties children have with maths include:

- Having difficulty remembering and recalling basic number sequences, patterns and number facts.

- Not being able to make connections between the word 'seven' and the number 7.

- Finding it difficult to count reliably, even when using manipulatives (cubes, pencils, counters, bead strings, etc.).

- Getting confused about which operation to use when working out a number equation, whether this be addition, subtraction, multiplication or division.

- Being unable to think of other ways to solve a problem, often only coming up with one solution, as to them it is the only way of completing the task.

- Difficulty in sorting objects or shapes based on their characteristics: shape, colour, properties, etc.

Funny story

I was once working with a child who had short-term memory issues, and the Ed Psych who had been observing her had told me that her memory was just like a filing cabinet, where someone had taken all of the files and thrown them up in the air (all of the information was in her head, but the child had to search longer than other children to find the right answer). I started to play some sorting games with her. The pictures I gave her were: a princess, a queen, a king, a polar bear, a penguin and a cat. I gave her these pictures and asked her to sort them and tell me why she had sorted them in this way. She studied every picture carefully. After a good ten minutes she had sorted them. In one column there were the princess, the queen, the king and the penguin and in the other column were the polar bear and cat. I asked her why she had put them into those categories. The child told me that the first column all contained things to do with the royal family. I asked her to explain her answer a little more. She said the queen, the king, the princess and the *emperor* penguin were all words used to describe people in royal families, whilst the second column was just made up of animals. I don't think I have ever felt so guilty for underestimating a child in my life.

When working with an individual or small group of children who have difficulty with certain areas of maths, or just certain areas, it can be very challenging, as you think you must be teaching the children incorrectly or you are not good at explaining a particular concept. There are things you can try, however, and I hope you will try some of these with the children you work with:

Tips

Tip 1: Use sorting activities, where children have to sort objects or shapes based on certain characteristics. At first, you can give the children the characteristics (e.g. sort these objects into green and blue) but as they grow in confidence, the children can begin to identify which characteristics they have used to sort the objects.

Tip 2: Introduce the children to a range of ways to carry out a task, but make sure they are secure before moving on. Find out which method the child feels comfortable with and then stick to this in future lessons.

Tip 3: Play lots of matching games, where the children are encouraged to match the number written as a numeral and objects that match the number.

Tip 4: Provide lots of opportunities for the children to practise their counting skills; for example, counting steps as they move around the setting, counting how many teachers or children they encounter during their journey from the classroom to the playground or recognising numbers around the setting. Room numbers and barcode numbers in the library are just some of the ways a child can be exposed to number.

Tip 5: Use the IWB to introduce the children to different number games where a wide range of mathematical topics can be introduced and practised (number recognition, counting, ordering, measuring, etc.).

There may be times when, despite whatever you have tried, the child is still finding maths difficult (and at times impossible). If this happens (and it will) it may be necessary to speak to other colleagues who may have supported a child with dyscalculia previously or the SENDCo. Both will be able to offer ideas of what has worked for other children they have supported with similar difficulties. However, you need to remember that what might have helped one child may not help the child you are supporting at all. If all else fails, the child may need to be referred to PSS, who are professionals who come into the setting to assess the child and devise an individualised plan to support the child. Once the setting have implemented the plan (usually through one-to-one support by the TA) the child is then regularly assessed by the practitioner from PSS to see if the programme is working and new targets need to be set, or if the child is struggling and even more interventions must be implemented.

Transition

Throughout primary education children go through many periods of transition: moving classes at the end of the academic year; moving between classrooms for core subjects (if they are being taught by different teachers); when making the move from Key Stage 1 (KS1) to

Key Stage 2 (KS2); and when leaving primary education altogether, to name but a few. The way these periods of change are managed is very important (and this is where your expertise may be required again). Children like the structure and familiarity that a primary setting provides, and they can get worried and nervous (just as adults can) when they need to move on or go somewhere new; but children with SEN (especially those with autism) are especially susceptible to this, and so they really need to be thought about during this process.

As part of your role, you may be asked to prepare children for the up-and-coming change (whatever this may be). In order to support the transition properly, the setting must make sure that the staff who support the child and know the children well have a good knowledge of the effects transition can have on the child. The setting must also supply the necessary resources for the staff to support the children throughout the whole transition – before, during and after the transition if necessary. Transition or change within the setting can be an incredibly stressful time for children, and coping with it for the first time can be demanding. Don't be afraid to ask the setting for support and training for yourself during these times, which will give you a clear understanding of the stresses the children may experience and how you can support them. Some of the strategies that may help during a period of transition include:

> **Tips**
>
> **Tip 1:** Talk to the children about the new situation or place in a positive way, well before they make the transition, to prepare the children for the changes that will happen.
>
> **Tip 2:** Ask the children what they are worried about and give them plenty of opportunities to ask questions (put a question box in the classroom; have a question wall where children put up their worries anonymously on sticky notes). You will be surprised how relieved the other children will be that someone has asked the question they may have been too embarrassed to ask. *If nobody puts any questions in the box, you can always add questions you think children may like the answers to. The children do not need to know it was you who wrote the questions.
>
> **Tip 3:** Organise some transition visits to the new classroom or secondary school if possible, so the children can get a feel for the new setting.
>
> **Tip 4:** Produce a transition book with photographs of the setting, people from the setting and the important places in the setting. *If moving from

primary to secondary, it may be necessary to introduce children to the new timings of the new setting; new lessons they may encounter; the behavioural expectations; and the need to become more independent (getting equipment ready and completing homework on time).

SEND Code of Practice

Over the last two years there have been many changes to the process children have to go through when a special educational need is suspected. The reason I use the word 'suspected' is based on the fact that we are not medical practitioners, and it is not part of our role to diagnose children. Before the new SEND Code of Practice was introduced in 2014, a TA would ask the SENDCo within the setting for support. After a brief assessment, the TA would then be asked to either run a small intervention group or take the child out of the classroom and work with them on a one-to-one basis. This would have resulted in the child being assessed as School Action (SA). This stage of the process has now been removed, and the teacher is expected to plan for all children within the lessons to ensure they can fully access the curriculum. In order to do this effectively, the setting may need to make changes to provision and adult support, so that the children can participate in every aspect of school life.

However, if the needs of the child cannot be met by the setting, the SENDCo may decide to involve outside agencies and start the 'statementing' process. Although children new to the system are now given education, care and health plans (ECHPs), children in your setting may still have a statement until they reach secondary school, where they will be moved onto an ECHP as soon as possible. I hope that the diagram on the next page will help show what procedures need to be followed when a special educational need is identified.

As with everything in education, the correct procedures have to be followed; and looking at entitlement and provision for children with special educational needs and disabilities is no different. But it is important to remember that this process can be extremely stressful for both the child and the parents, and they will require lots of support from the setting during this time. You may need to go through the process with the parents many times and answer lots of questions, as it can be a very confusing time. Talking to the parents regularly and keeping them informed at every stage

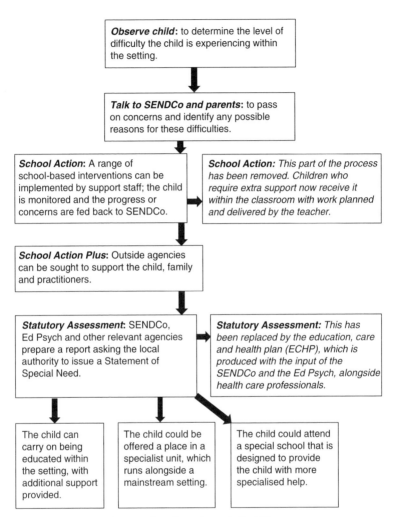

Observe child: to determine the level of difficulty the child is experiencing within the setting.

Talk to SENDCo and parents: to pass on concerns and identify any possible reasons for these difficulties.

School Action: A range of school-based interventions can be implemented by support staff; the child is monitored and the progress or concerns are fed back to SENDCo.

School Action: This part of the process has been removed. Children who require extra support now receive it within the classroom with work planned and delivered by the teacher.

School Action Plus: Outside agencies can be sought to support the child, family and practitioners.

Statutory Assessment: SENDCo, Ed Psych and other relevant agencies prepare a report asking the local authority to issue a Statement of Special Need.

Statutory Assessment: This has been replaced by the education, care and health plan (ECHP), which is produced with the input of the SENDCo and the Ed Psych, alongside health care professionals.

The child can carry on being educated within the setting, with additional support provided.

The child could be offered a place in a specialist unit, which runs alongside a mainstream setting.

The child could attend a special school that is designed to provide the child with more specialised help.

Special educational needs and disability process

of the process can put their minds at ease, making it easier to accept the help offered. However, at times, it is easy to forget about the parent and go ahead and make a decision that you feel is in the best interests of the child (if you do not want what is best for the child, then you are in the wrong job). But this simply cannot happen, as this can often end up causing ill feeling and damaging the relationship between the parents and the school. This, in turn, can have a devastating effect on the provision the child may receive (as the parent will not allow the child to work with staff who they feel are not involving them in their child's education). There are many different ways to make sure parents are kept well informed; these are just some of the methods I have tried over the years:

Tips

Tip 1: Phone or write a letter to the parents inviting them into the setting to discuss any issues or problems that have arisen. However, be mindful that English may not be the first language spoken at home; it may be necessary to translate the letter or ask someone who can speak the child's home language to phone home on your behalf.

Tip 2: Introduce a home/school book for parents to write in any concerns they may have. You (under the direction of the teacher) can then respond to these concerns.

Tip 3: Hold regular individual education plan (IEP) or individual behaviour plan (IBP) meetings, to give the parents up-to-date information on the progress being made by their child, the support they are receiving from the setting, and what external agencies are involved in meeting the needs of the child.

As well as keeping the parents informed, it is important to involve the child in the decision-making process, especially when deciding on the type of support they receive. However, you really do have to think about how you involve the child in the process and you also need to make sure that the methods used are appropriate to the age and needs of the child. Some ideas you may like to try are:

Tips

Tip 1: If the child is non-verbal, pictures or words can be used to give the child the opportunity to have their say about which parts of the provision they like; which parts they dislike; and what needs to be improved.

Tip 2: Talk to the child before any meetings to gain their views on how the provision is going; how they are getting on in the lessons; what they struggle with; who helps them to succeed; and what or who might support them further (really important when target-setting).

Tip 3: Invite the child to the IEP or IBP meetings so that they are able to voice their opinions in front of their parents; this sometimes empowers children to voice their views in a more open way than usual.

Tip 4: Write a child-friendly version of the IEP or IBP, so the child and staff can refer to it as and when needed.

Changes

Since the new legislation has come in, the way the process is funded has changed. Previously, when a child was given a statement, the school received a 'pot of money' that was used by the setting to meet the needs of the child, in the way they thought best. However, under the new guidelines, parents are now being given the option to hold the funding and spend it on the education and outside agency support they think their child needs. I must say (from talking to many SENDCos) that most parents have opted to keep the money under the control of the setting; parents feel the professionals in the setting really do want what is best for the child. Although funding is not part of the role of a TA, you do need to know about it, should a parent come and ask you how it works. However, if you are unsure, it may be necessary to speak to the SENDCo, to make sure you give parents the most relevant and up-to-date information.

As well as the process children have to go through, there have also been changes made to the terminology used around SEN. Here is just some of the wording that has changed:

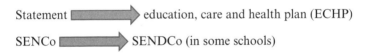

Statement ➤ education, care and health plan (ECHP)

SENCo ➤ SENDCo (in some schools)

I know that I have not written about all of the SEND you will see in every primary setting, but I hope this chapter has helped you to get to grips with some of the technical jargon used in primary settings and has provided you with lots of ideas and practical activities to try with the children you work with.

Chapter 3
Supporting children with English as an additional language

Over the last five years, there has been a massive influx of children who have entered the setting where I work who are either not able to speak English at all or who have a very limited understanding of the most basic English. It is now one of the most diverse settings within an inner-city school, with children speaking a wide range of languages (31 in all), with the most common languages spoken by the children being English, Punjabi, Urdu and Romanian. However, this issue is not specific to Birmingham; it is also happening in many primary settings throughout the United Kingdom.

Welcoming a child with EAL into the setting

One of the most important things to remember when a child with EAL enters the classroom (and they will) is just how frightened and worried the child will be when entering the setting for the first time (especially if they are the only child who speaks their language). I think it is easy for us to underestimate just how scary this experience must be, especially when the child is not able to tell anyone:

- how they feel
- whether they have understood what is being asked of them

- if they need help and support
- that they need to have the instruction repeated or explained to them again
- about something that they have enjoyed in the school day
- about an issue they may be experiencing.

When a child or children enter the setting with English as an additional language (EAL), it is often the TA who will greet the child and accompany them to their new classroom; this will ensure the child gets a calm and stress-free start to their day. As the child starts to settle, you (as the TA) will often be the member of staff who will introduce them to the teaching and support staff, routines and expectations of the setting.

Once the child has settled in, it will be up to the teacher to carry out basic assessments of reading and writing in both English and the child's home language to build up a picture of what the child already knows and where the gaps in their learning are. This initial assessment will allow you to gain an idea of what interventions may need to be put in place to support the child to best meet their needs. Although the ultimate aim is to provide the child with an education, this can only be achieved once the child feels relaxed and comfortable within the setting; so, initially, this takes priority. Therefore, it is up to you (in partnership with the class teacher of course) to make the child feel like part of the class as soon as possible. If this is achieved, it can make a real difference to the progress the child will make during their time in the setting with their social and academic skills.

At first, the prospect of supporting a child or a small group of children with EAL can be quite daunting, as you suddenly become aware of just how little you know about other cultures and languages. But there are many strategies that can help, so there is no need to worry. One of the first suggestions I would make is to read the English as an additional language (EAL) policy (which may be included in the SEND policy), as it will clearly set out the procedures that should be followed when a child with EAL enters the setting. If things are not clear, then it may be necessary for you to talk to the SENDCo, as they will be able to provide you with a variety of resources that can be used to meet the needs of the child (whatever these may be). It may also be useful to speak to other TAs who have supported children with EAL, as they will definitely be able to share with you the type of games and activities that have been used successfully in the past. Bilingual staff (if you are lucky enough to have them) are also an amazing source of information, and some of these will be able to interpret if and when needed (especially if the child is getting upset or not understanding what is being asked of them in their first few days at the setting). During my time as a TA, I have had the pleasure of supporting many children from a variety of countries and who have spoken many different languages. I can honestly say that while it can be initially overwhelming (for a first-timer), once you build up a relationship with the child (and they start to understand your 'dodgy' hand gestures and facial expressions) you will be surprised how quickly the child will start to communicate with you. Some of the activities I have used with children when welcoming them into the setting for the very first time include:

Tips

Tip 1: Produce a welcome pack – to include: photographs of people they may meet in the setting (teacher, TA, head teacher, deputy head); places the child may visit during the school day (school office, library, playground and canteen); and the names and pictures of common objects the child may need to use during the day (rubber, table, chair, pen, pencil and book). It is also beneficial to provide the labels in English and the home language, not only to help the child to understand the names of important people and objects in and around the setting, but also to encourage the parents to support their child at home.

Tip 2: Label equipment around the classroom in dual languages (English and home language). *If the equipment could be labelled in the home language (with the child's help), then it can have a really positive impact on the child, as they will feel that you not only value their language but have also taken the time to find out about their language and country of origin.

Tip 3: Use the Internet to find out some common words in the home language: greetings, colours, days of the week and months of the year are always a good place to start. Spending a small amount of time finding these will be worth it in the long run, as the child will soon start to feel more settled and as if they have a link to home.

Tip 4: Make up an 'EAL' assessment pack in which the child can show you how to write their name, what their likes and dislikes are and who lives in the house with them. If the process is proving stressful for the child, it is fine, at this stage, to encourage the child to draw, rather than write, the required information.

Practical ideas

Make sure you attend any meetings that take place with the parents and child before they actually start the setting. These informal get-togethers can be so beneficial, as they can provide you with the opportunity to find out information that may help you support the child in the lessons (what understanding the child has in the home language; what the child enjoys outside of school; what they find difficult) and identify ways the setting can support the child and family.

Try to sit the child next to someone who is going to make them feel welcome (and who speaks their home language, if possible). However, if this is not possible, then you may be able to find someone in the setting with whom they can communicate, as this can make the settling-in period far easier.

Making friends

Not being able to speak English must be an extremely frightening time for a child with EAL and can often result in the child feeling isolated and apprehensive at the prospect of meeting children with whom they simply cannot communicate. But with your skilled input, the child will soon feel like part of the class. Often, talking to the class before the child arrives can help them settle in quickly, as classmates will have the opportunity to ask questions they cannot ask once the child joins the class: Where is the child from? Has the child been to school before? Why hasn't the child been to school before? What language do they speak? A class discussion may also give the class a chance to think about how they could welcome the child, who may want to support the child on their first day, and how they could greet the child when they first enter the classroom.

Tips

Tip 1: Teach the children in your class how to greet the new child in their home language; this will not only make the new arrival feel welcome, but will also teach the children a new skill.

Tip 2: Set up a 'buddy system' where a child (who speaks the same language, if possible) can show the new child around the setting, answering any questions or concerns they may have.

Tip 3: Set up a friendship group, which will encourage the child to talk to others and join in any games they are playing. Card games and board games are a really good resource to invest in, as the rules are pretty self-explanatory and are quickly picked up by everyone, regardless of language skills.

Tip 4: Use role play to explore how the child may have felt when entering the setting for the first time. Drama is a really effective way to get children to talk about topics they may not necessarily like to talk about normally. It not only provides children with the opportunity to find out how difficult and stressful new situations can be, but also allows them to try out different strategies that may be used to alleviate any stress felt.

In most cases, you will find that children are very accepting of other children who enter the setting and will make friends with the child. There may be times when a child may find it difficult to fit into the class and be accepted by the children in the setting. It is possible that some children within the setting have negative attitudes towards children from different countries, cultures or religions (for whatever reason). Therefore, it is up to you to watch how the other children react to the new arrival and challenge their views, if needed. In order for the children to air their feelings in a safe environment and resolve any issues or misunderstandings, you may suggest to the teacher that a circle time take place. During the session, children should be encouraged to ask questions about the child (culture and language). However, if the issues persist, it may be necessary to contact the parents, so the source of these thoughts and feelings can be discussed further.

Welcoming parents

As well as making the children feel welcome, you will also need to spend some time building up good relationships with parents, so they feel able to come into the setting if they should need to talk to you about their child. The language barrier can be a bit daunting at first, but the more you speak and get to know them, the more confident you (and the parent) will become. Working alongside parents will be a big part of your role as a TA, as you will often be the person who greets the parents and child as they enter the classroom, so you really do need to take advantage of opportunities to talk to parents as and when they arise.

Tips

Tip 1: Speak to the parents before the child enters the setting to find out what language the child speaks at home and what their levels of understanding are in their home language (don't forget; you may need to take an interpreter with you).

Tip 2: Produce a welcome booklet, which will introduce children (and parents) with EAL to: school staff, places of importance within the school, the school office, canteen, library, ICT suite, etc. Make sure the photographs and captions are clear, and refer to them as the child is moving around the setting.

Tip 3: Make a picture book full of common objects the child will see during the school day; pencil, pen, table, chair, door and coat peg are just some of the words that could be included. A really good way to encourage the child to say the words is to label them in the home language and English; this will help the child make links between a new language and the language they are more familiar with. If a child speaks Romanian, then the following may help (but you can adapt it to any language):

|  | creion (Romanian) | pencil (English) |

Tip 4: Never underestimate the importance of the home language; use any opportunity to refer back to the language the child is confident in.

Practical ideas

Organise an informal 'get-together' for new and existing parents, which will give them the opportunity to make new friends, ask any questions about the setting and become part of the school community. Other parents may also be able to talk to the new arrivals about help and support that is available from the wider community, e.g. doctors, health visitors or play groups, to name but a few.

Invite the parents to come into the classroom and label the objects in their home language. *By welcoming the child and the parents into the setting, the child will feel as though their language is valued and you will be able to develop a really strong home–school link, both of which can have an extremely positive impact on the child's and parents' self-esteem.

If possible, translate letters that are being sent home into the home language, so that parents are kept fully informed about what is going on in the setting and do not feel left out. *This may not be possible if there are lots of different languages spoken by the parents.

Ask bilingual staff to be on hand at important times of the day, e.g. at the start of the day, at home time and during parents evening, so that parents can be informed of anything they may need to know and information can be exchanged between school and home, e.g. positive comments about the child and their work, concerns about their child and/or anything else the parent may need to know about the school day.

Introducing the child to the school day

During any school day all children are given lots of information by many different people in the setting: in assemblies, in the canteen and around the school in general. Just some of the examples that come to mind include: the head teacher telling the children about a new school initiative or making sure the children know how to stay safe, or the dinner supervisors making an announcement about the dinnertime rotas or playground safety, to name but a few. Important information is also given out in the classrooms, which the child needs to be able to understand:

- explanations of a new concept
- instructions for a task
- messages they may need to pass on to their parents or another member of staff.

If the child is not supported during these times, the child can become worried and scared, as they will not know what has been said and how it will affect them. Therefore, it may be necessary to work alongside the teacher and SENDCo to devise strategies that may help the child access some of the language used in and around the setting.

One such strategy, which is particularly effective, is to use very simple language when the child first comes into the classroom, especially when they have little or no English at all (you may also need to show the children what you mean through pictures). There is no point in speaking in full sentences; this will just confuse the child. It is far better to talk to the child in a word or short phrase with lots of hand gestures to get the child to understand what is being asked of them. For example, if you need to get a child to write in pencil, it may be necessary to just say 'pencil' and hold up a pencil. When the child follows the instruction successfully, it is important that you acknowledge it straight away with a reward (whichever rewards are used within the setting: merits, stickers, smiley faces or a simple 'thumbs up' are always good starting points). By rewarding the positive behaviour, the child is more likely to 'have a go' when asked to do something else in the future. As the child grows in confidence and gains more vocabulary, you will need to use more words and eventually move on to speaking in short sentences. In time, the child may be able to use most of the new words correctly; however, the child may still make mistakes with meanings and pronunciation. To help the child develop a better understanding of the English language, you may need to explain any misconceptions and correct any mistakes made by slowly repeating the correct pronunciation of the word back to the child a few times. But once the child has understood what you have said, they will start to experiment with using it in other contexts (and when they do, remember it was you that taught them how to do it).

Tips

Tip 1: Give the child a feelings sliding scale, so the child can let you know how they feel at different times of the school day. It may sound simple (and it is) but it a really easy way to find out how the child is feeling, without the child having to think of the language needed to describe how they are feeling and why.

Tip 2: Give the child a feelings lanyard, which they can show to staff if they are unable to verbalise their feelings.

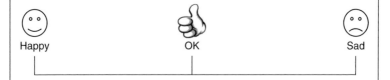

Happy   OK   Sad

Tip 3: Use flashcards with the child with EAL, which will introduce them to common words that they encounter during the day; days of the week, months of the year and keywords are just some of the words that may benefit the child.

Tip 4: Make sure you model good English to the child, so the child gets the correct pronunciation of the word 'first time'. However, this can often be very confusing when working in inner-city Birmingham, as there are many different dialects in and around the local area. (At this point, I think it is important to tell you I am a Yam Yam. For those of you who don't know what this means, I am from the Black Country; I can hear you all doing your best Dudley accent as I write this.)

Learning through play

Another way to encourage language is through play. All children learn in different ways, but I have always found that children with EAL tend to pick up the new language more effectively if it is introduced in a fun way. Believe me, I know how difficult it is to find the time during your already packed day, but once you have made the resources, games and activities, you can re-use them with other children with EAL (if and when needed).

Initially, the child might stand on the outskirts of the playground watching the children playing and gauging what is expected from all of the players. Children from the class may approach the child and try to get them to join in the game, but even then the child will often refuse, as they fear they may not be able to play the game properly. However, once the child does take up the offer to play with others (and they will, it may just take a while), the child will often quickly begin to copy the words and phrases the other children say. As the child becomes more confident, they may start to show the other children how to play games (games they have played in their native country). At this point, it may also be beneficial to introduce the child to team games, which can really engage a child who may be struggling during the more formal parts of the day (registration, lessons and assemblies) to make friends with some of the other children in the class. You will be surprised at how fast the child will make friends and how quickly they will learn popular key words and phrases. 'Cool' or 'Your shoes are sick!' are just some of the words and phrases children new to the English language tend to pick up pretty quickly. The first time you hear a child with little or no English saying these phrases will sound a little strange, but it is also quite encouraging to know that they must have been talking to other children in order to pick up these new words.

Funny story

A few years ago a new child came into the setting from Nepal and only spoke Nepalese. We used Google Translate to greet the child and typed in sentences that the child could respond to (which helped the child a lot with communicating his thoughts and ideas). After a few weeks, I asked the child a maths question, which he got wrong. He put his hand on top of his head and said, 'D-oh!' He then said, 'Bart told me English.' I was really impressed that *The Simpsons* had taught the child English so quickly and the child had picked it up and used it in the right context.

Although watching *The Simpsons* is good fun, there are far more effective strategies that can be used to introduce children to new words and phrases:

Tips

Tip 1: Set up a 'games club' (indoors) which children can access during the playtimes and dinnertimes if they feel anxious about going into the playground with other children. Initially, the child may wish to pick a friend they feel comfortable to go with, but as the child grows in confidence they may choose to attend the club on their own or with a wider group of friends.

Tip 2: Take a small group of children (who can model good turn-taking and 'play by the rules') into the playground to play games; skipping games are a very good way to encourage social interaction, as are giant outdoor games such as snakes and ladders and Jenga®. These types of games are also really beneficial, as they encourage the child to take turns and give them the opportunity to make new and exciting friendships.

Tip 3: Introduce a 'buddy system' so the children can compete against each other; name pictures the fastest and point to the 'animal' the quickest are just some of the games that can be used to encourage language and word recognition. Using the children's competitive streak (and I truly believe that all children have this to some extent) will encourage the child to experiment with the new language and communication skills they have learnt, in a safe and supportive environment.

Expressing ideas, thoughts and feelings

Everyone needs to express their thoughts and feelings at one time or another. But children with EAL can find this extremely problematic, as they simply do not have the language needed to name their emotions. As well as the language, children also need to master the use of correct facial expressions, hand gestures and eye contact; all of these need to be mastered if the child is going to be able to communicate effectively. Therefore, it may be necessary for you to model the appropriate emotions and name the feelings so the child knows what these are and when it is appropriate to use them. However, before you do this, it is important to research what expressions and hand gestures are used in the country the child has come from, to make sure none of the gestures that are acceptable in the UK mean something different to the child (we would not want anyone to be offended).

Helping children through this confusing time of reading facial expressions and looking for clues about how they are feeling can sometimes feel overwhelming. Even now, there are times when I just do not know how the child is ever going to make friends and fit in. But, as I have said many times throughout the book, there are many people you can ask for help; the SENDCo and other colleagues are always the first people I go to. Talking to the parents can also be extremely helpful, as they will often have a clear picture of how the child feels about the setting. Parents will know whether their child is settling in well, if the child is experiencing any issues, what the child enjoys or anything that may be making the child feel anxious. Here are just some of the strategies that I have used to help support children with EAL to express their thoughts and feelings:

Tips

Tip 1: Play games around feelings and emotions with all of the children in the class, at times when you might have five minutes spare (it does happen sometimes – honest!). The children love nothing better than acting out emotions, especially being angry, sad, excited and heartbroken, while the rest of the class guess which emotion is being played out. The classes I currently work with love the word 'heartbroken' and use it at many different times throughout the day.

Tip 2: Take out a small group of children to a quiet area (six children – two EAL children and four children who are really confident when talking about their feelings). Split the children into pairs and give one of the children a mirror and give the other child the name of an emotion they have to show to their partner. But before they show their partner you must give them time to practise this emotion in the mirror. The partner must then guess which emotion the child is trying to express. The game not only encourages the child to recognise and name different emotions, but also gives the child the opportunity to pull funny faces in the mirror, which in turn helps them to build friendships in a fun way. *Take pictures of the group showing different emotions, which you can refer to if the child is feeling sad, upset, excited or happy.

Tip 3: Use PSHE time to discuss scenarios that encourage the children to think about how they would feel in certain situations, e.g. starting a new school, being left out of a game in the playground or being pressured into doing something they know is wrong by their 'friends'.

Tip 4: Give the child a 'feelings' lanyard (KS2), to wear around the neck, so the child can show someone how they are feeling if they have not yet got the language to express this verbally. If used with younger children, it is important to buy the lanyards with the straps that release when pulled (to stop the possibility of strangulation).

Practical ideas

Have a feelings chart up on the classroom door, so all children have the opportunity to say how they are feeling as they enter the classroom. Give all children access to a smiley face, sad face, a straight face and a face that can be customised with a dry marker pen, so the child can show you if they feel any other emotion (maybe they feel excited as their birthday is coming up shortly, or angry as they have had an argument with their little brother before school).

Get the children in the class to make faces showing different emotions, which can be put up around the classroom and referred to as and when needed. Having these resources readily available will give the child the opportunity to let you know how they are feeling instantly.

Create a set of 'snap cards' of feelings words and the matching pictures. The cards can then be used in a variety of ways: matching the picture to the correct word; as a 'snap'-type game; or where the child has to pick up a card in response to a scenario you give them. *The first time the child is able to describe their feelings or the feelings of others will fill you with a great sense of pride, which will make all of the hard work seem worth it.

Praise

Some children cannot take a compliment, but the majority of children respond well to positive praise. When a child with EAL first enters the setting, one of the ways you can reinforce what you need them to do is by using lots of hand gestures, such as clapping and thumbs up when they are successful (whether it be for following an instruction first time, attempting to answer a question in a small group or class situation or trying to join in during a lesson). There is no point in telling the child how proud you are of them or that their work is amazing because they will simply not be able to understand what you are pleased about (even if you use your best smile). However, as the child begins to gain in confidence and understanding, you may begin to use words or phrases such as 'good' and 'well done', along with stickers and smiley faces to reinforce the feelings of happiness. If this praise is given straight away, and you make it really clear to the child why you are so happy with them, then they are more likely to repeat the action again, in order to receive the praise again.

Tips

Tip 1: Design a reward chart with the child, making sure you give the child the opportunity to add pictures of their favourite cartoon characters, football players or family members around the edges. By including the child's interests on the reward chart, you will not only make the chart more personal to them but also make the child more likely to want to fill up the chart with positive comments.

Tip 2: Make sure the reward chart, smiley face chart or house point chart (whichever rewards are featured in your setting's behaviour policy) is placed somewhere visible, to encourage the child to try their best even when they are finding the set task challenging.

Tip 3: Remember to use verbal praise (alongside the corresponding facial expressions), so the child can clearly see you are happy with them.

Tip 4: Give the child the opportunity to 'show off' work they are proud of to their peers. It may not be of the same standards as their peers, but it will boost their confidence no end.

However, one thing I have found during my time as a TA is that children need to know what type of behaviour earns them praise and rewards. If all staff within the setting use different methods to reward good behaviour, then the child can get confused. To avoid any confusion, I suggest you take the time to read the behaviour policy, so that you are clear about the methods of praise that should be used to reward the children with EAL. If this is unclear, then it may be necessary to arrange a meeting with either the phase leader or year group leader to discuss this further. There is nothing wrong with asking SMT to clarify issues that you are unsure about – just ask.

Accessing the curriculum

Once the child has had a chance to settle in and the level of support the child needs is determined, it may be necessary for you to work alongside a child at various points during the day, so they can take an active part in the lessons. This can be extremely difficult and stressful at times, especially when you are expected to introduce the child to the rules and routines of the settings and the curriculum as soon as possible (so the child can meet the government's targets). Initially, it may be necessary to carry out some 'pre-tutoring'. (Do not worry – this is not as scary as it sounds.) It is a chance for you to introduce the child to language they will encounter in the lesson and make it easier for the child to access the lesson at a later date.

However, there may be times when the child does not understand what is being asked of them. If this happens, then it is time to use your amazing TA skills again. You will soon get into the habit of using the most ingenious ways of getting your point across (it will amaze you how much 'sign language' you have). The use of hand gestures and facial expressions (no matter how bad) are so important during the initial lessons, as they will let the children know what they need to do and how successful they are being. I have already talked about the benefit of positive praise, but it is so important to smile a lot when teaching a new topic, as it helps the child know you are there for them and feel confident you will be able to help and support them if and when needed. But there may be times when you feel you have tried 'everything' to get the child to understand a new concept or topic, and nothing seems to work. If you get to this point (and we all do; it is not just you) then do not be afraid to ask your colleagues for help. Most TAs will have had experience of supporting children with EAL to some degree, and will be able to provide you with some great ideas and activities that can be used to support children to understand and use English effectively. However, there will also be activities that should be avoided, as they have little or no impact at all. There will also be many bilingual staff in the setting who can explain something to the child if they are finding something difficult to understand.

Tips

Tip 1: Use TA websites (as previously mentioned) to prepare pictorial clues and basic words and phrases that will support the child and their understanding of a new topic or vocabulary.

Tip 2: Try to carry out the lessons as practically as possible, in order for the child to 'have a go' and see what happens, instead of being told what the outcome is going to be. Science, design and technology (DT) and, of course, maths are all subjects where practical apparatus can be used to explore concepts.

Tip 3: Ask bilingual staff if they are able to come and explain the new topic or concept in the home language before the lesson, so the child will have a basic understanding of what is being asked of them.

Tip 4: Produce a checklist to support the child with keeping a check on where they are in the lesson and what they need to do next.

As I am writing this, I have just been informed that I have a new child joining my teaching group later on this week. The child has never attended a school in England and only speaks Dutch. After the initial shock of another child with EAL joining my group ten weeks before SATS, my TA brain has gone into overdrive about all of the things I need to prepare in such a short amount of time: timetables in the home language (with pictures); labels in dual languages (English and Dutch); and, of course, my trusty 'welcome pack'.

Although it is easy to feel sorry for the child or children coming into the setting for the very first time, the more experience you have of working with children with EAL, the more confident you will be in your ability to provide them with the help and support they need. The progress the child or children make will seem like baby steps at times, but when you take the opportunity to look back at the end of the academic year, you will quickly realise that the improvement the children have made is massive when compared to the other children in the year group. It will also become apparent that, at times, the child has taken the role of the teacher, to teach us about their language and culture. Supporting children with EAL is a very satisfying part of my role and one of the many reasons I love being a teaching assistant.

Funny story

A couple of years ago, another TA and I were told that a new child was coming into the class on Monday. We asked what we knew about the child. The only thing the administration staff could tell us was that the child had not been to school in England before and was only able to speak limited English. I asked what language the child spoke at home and was told 'he's Romanian'. On hearing this, we both went into overdrive and started to get resources ready, and thought we were being really clever by using Google Translate.

The child came into the setting on Monday and we welcomed him and then went to show him that we could welcome him in Romanian as well as English. We played the translation and the child looked confused, so we played it again. The child looked even more confused. We said 'hello' and waved at the child frantically. He waved back, but must have thought we were mad. He said, 'I sorry, I do not understand.' We told the child that the computer had taught us Romanian, but the child kept on saying 'no'. We then looked on the form to check which language the child spoke. It was then that we realised that he spoke Roma, which is totally different from Romanian. At least the child came into the setting and knew we had made an effort to welcome him, albeit in the wrong language.

Now I have shared my experience of working alongside children with EAL, just take a minute to think about a child you have met or worked with who speaks EAL. Imagine you have been sent to a setting where you are the only person who speaks a different language. All of the information given to you is in a language you do not understand. What a scary and frightening experience this would be (some of the children in the setting will be experiencing this all day, every day). I hope reading this chapter has helped you realise what an important role you play in supporting a child or children with EAL.

Chapter 4
Supporting children with behavioural issues

During any given day or lesson, you may be faced with a child (or children) who show unacceptable behaviour for whatever reason. Therefore, before you even enter the classroom, I strongly suggest you take the time to read through the behaviour policy. This will give you a clear idea of the procedures that should be followed if a child is showing unacceptable behaviour in and around the setting, and the expectations of behaviour that staff should have within the setting.

Sometimes the reasons for the unwanted behaviour are immediately obvious and you can clearly see why the child has become distressed. The child may have:

- found the work too difficult

- argued with friends at playtime or dinnertime

- been asked to complete a task that the child does not want to do (being asked to work with a child of the opposite sex can often be the cause of much upset, especially when the child reaches Year 5 or 6)

- experienced an unexpected change (perhaps the class teacher is ill and a supply teacher has been asked to cover the class)

- been required to move classes for certain lessons (this only tends to happen if a teacher only teaches a certain subject)

- been irritated by another child (who may have said something negative to them or used intimidating body language).

However, there may be occasions when the reason for the unacceptable behaviour is not so obvious. The child may have:

- family issues (bereavement of a family member or family pet, separation, divorce, abuse or domestic violence)
- an issue with a particular teacher and feels unable to speak out about it for fear of getting into trouble
- a problem with one of the lessons, but is scared of the consequences if they raise a complaint
- the feeling that something has happened that they think is unfair.

If this is the case, you may need to use all of your communication (and detective) skills to try to find out what is going on. I always tell children, 'I cannot help you sort out the problem if you do not tell me what is going on'. By not putting too much pressure on the child, he or she may feel as though they have been given 'permission' to open up and talk about any problems they are experiencing. Also, if you have managed to build up a professional bond with the child from the beginning, the child will be more willing to open up to you in these types of situations. When talking about feelings, there is always the potential for a 'disclosure' to be made, regarding some type of abuse (whether this is physical or emotional) that the child is experiencing. Therefore, it is extremely important to have this at the back of your mind when dealing with such issues; make sure you are in a room where you are clearly visible to other members of staff, and never promise the child you can keep a secret they tell you. These are just two of the ways you can help keep the child and yourself safe.

Practical ideas

Have a 'concerns book' available to write down any issues that have been raised by the child, so they know their views have been noted. Recording these incidents will help you keep track of ongoing conflicts between certain children and could (if the problems persist) indicate a deeper issue that may need further investigation.

I know I have said this many times throughout the book, but in order for a child to learn effectively, the child needs to feel valued, accepted as a member of the class and, above all, happy. In order for this to happen, the relationship between you and the teacher needs to work well. A healthy teacher–TA relationship can have a massive impact on the children and how they feel in both the classroom and the setting in general (especially in relation to whether they feel happy and safe enough to learn effectively).

Rewards

During the day, there will be times when a child does something that simply makes your jaw drop: maybe the child has been able to complete a task they have never been able to finish before; or has attempted to answer a question in a whole-class situation; or has brought in extra research they have completed at home (or just simply gone above and beyond what you have asked of them). In order to let the child know you are happy with what they have done, you must give the child a reward. But, before you do this, I would suggest you take the time to read the rewards section of the setting's behaviour policy. This will clearly set out which rewards are used by the staff to encourage or show a positive attitude to their behaviour and learning. There are many behaviour management strategies that can be used either to reward the child for making the right choice or to encourage the behaviours the setting wants to see repeated. The most common rewards used in primary settings include:

- Smiley faces or merits, which children can collect and swap for prizes or certificates.

- Stickers placed on the child's work or clothing can be effective, as the parents and staff instantly know the child has done something positive and will ask them about it (resulting in the child receiving verbal praise as well).

- Privilege passes, which the child can use to gain extra playtime, time on the laptops, the chance to work alongside their friend for a lesson, or an art and craft session.

- 'I did well' stickers, which can be used by TA and teachers to highlight good work and behaviour. If members of staff see the child around the setting, they must ask the child what they did well. By doing this, the child can receive praise from a wide range of people, which will boost their self-esteem no end.

- 'Good work' certificates, which can be used to motivate even the most reluctant learners, especially if presented in a celebration assembly (see the Tips below).

- Send the child to the head teacher to receive a 'Head Teacher Award', which can be given if the child has produced a remarkable piece of work (for them) or achieved something extraordinary.

- Sometimes using simple verbal praise is enough for children (especially those in Early Years and KS1). It can also help to adjust the behaviour of the other children, as they see that they might also receive praise if they choose to 'do the right thing'.

Tips

Tip 1: Make sure you have a huge supply of certificates and stickers readily available. *The Education Shows that are held across the country annually are a really good place to buy these (sometimes these are given away free).

Tip 2: Give the child the rewards as soon as possible, to ensure maximum effect.

Tip 3: Tell the child why they have been chosen to receive a reward, so the child knows what behaviours need to be repeated in the future.

Tip 4: Use a reward that is appropriate to the age of the child. Some children will do anything for a sticker; others will not. But as you get to know the child, you will quickly establish which rewards are effective and which are not.

Tip 5: Award certificates can be given as part of a celebration assembly (where friends and family are invited to come and celebrate their achievements). These assemblies can have such a positive impact on the child and motivate even the most reluctant learner.

Funny story

I was working in a reception class many years ago, when one of the girls came up to me and told me she had been given a 'tercificate' by the teacher and that she was so, so excited about it. The child was talking so quickly and repeating it over and over again. But I could not understand what she was trying to tell me. I eventually asked the teacher why the girl was so animated. She told me that the girl had tried so hard with her phonics that she had given her a certificate. It was just so heart-warming that I have never forgotten it (even though it was about 15 years ago).

It is also important to be really clear why you have chosen to give the child the reward. By doing this, the child will associate the good behaviour with a reward and will be much more likely to repeat the desired behaviour again, in the hope of receiving another reward. However, over-using rewards can sometimes backfire, as some children will then only carry out the task based on the external reward they are going to receive, while others may even refuse to do the task until they have the promise of the reward at the end of it. (This is called bribery and corruption, and is not a good road to go down.) Therefore, you may need to use your imagination to motivate the child to show good behaviour and take an active part in their learning in other ways. For example, if you encourage the child to help others and make friends, the positive feedback they receive will make them feel good about themselves – a key factor in motivating them to learn.

Sanctions

Sanctions are no different to using rewards, but instead of being used for positive behaviours, they are usually used when the child has made the wrong choice (or when the child has shown unacceptable behaviour). The child may have refused to follow an instruction or been rude to another child or member of staff, to name but a few wrong choices. Children need to understand right from an early age that, if they do the wrong thing, there will be a consequence for their actions. The consequences again will form a major part of the behaviour policy, so make sure you are clear about what sanctions are used in the setting and which behaviours trigger their use. However, if these are to be used effectively, the child also needs to know (in advance) what the expectations are for attitude and behaviour in and around the setting, and which behaviours will earn them a consequence.

To other children	Towards their work	To a member of staff
Swearing	Not wanting to take part in a particular task	Using inappropriate language; swearing or answering back
Physically hurting; pinching, kicking and punching	Refusing to complete work	Not following an instruction that has been given
Using unacceptable verbal assaults (normally about the physical appearance of another child)	Scribbling over work in books when refusing to complete a task	Physically aggressive attitude; hitting or trying to intimidate

Although there is a possibility you may face some of these behaviours in your role as a TA, I feel it is necessary to make it clear (before you rethink your job choice) that most of these actions are not common in a primary setting. However, there is a range of strategies that can be used in a primary setting to show the child that a behaviour is unacceptable; these include:

- Losing all or part of outside time (either break time or dinnertime).

- Sending the child to a partner class, which can be used to give the child the chance to reflect on their 'wrong choice' of behaviour, or for completing their unfinished work in another class, where there may be fewer distractions.

- Speaking to members of the SMT about the need to speak to the child about their behaviour, how changes can be made, and the need to make better choices.

- Being sent straight to the head teacher's office. This is not normally necessary, as the strategies set out in the behaviour policy are usually enough to calm the child down. However, there are times when the behaviour shown is so extreme (when, for instance, the child is at risk of hurting themselves or others) that the head teacher must be informed.

At this point, depending on the severity of the behaviour shown by the child, it may be necessary to give the child an in-house exclusion or to even permanently exclude the child. If the head teacher decides that the child should receive an in-house exclusion, you may be asked to gather work for the day and take the child to a room where they will complete their work in isolation (away from their class). If this is part of your role, you may be required to escort the child as they move around the setting, i.e. accompany the child for a toilet break and during recreation time (often a short break in the playground to give the child a chance to get a breath of fresh air), and take them into the canteen to get dinner. Escorting the child to and from all the places they would normally go on their own cuts down the likelihood of the child getting themselves into even more trouble.

However, if the decision is made to permanently exclude the child, you may be asked to wait with the child until the parent is able to come and collect the child, or sit with the child whilst the parents are meeting with the head teacher. The decision to exclude a child (whether it is an in-house or permanent exclusion) is never taken lightly. It often comes as a result of the child showing such extreme behaviour in the setting that they have put either themselves or others (children and staff) in danger of harm, whether this be physical harm or a threat to their education (as a result of constant disruption).

At times, when dealing with such disturbing behaviour, it is hard to remain professional. But it is important to remember that children learn how to behave and respond appropriately from watching how responsible adults react to certain situations. So, always try to keep your anger and upset to a minimum (you can have a rant in the staffroom later) and make sure you label the *behaviour* as unacceptable and not the child. Phrases that can help include: 'The behaviour you have just shown me is not what I expect', 'You know that the behaviour you have just used is unacceptable, don't you?' and 'I cannot believe you have used that language; it is not an acceptable thing to say to someone, is it?' Labelling the child (as 'naughty', 'silly' or 'selfish') can have a devastating effect on the child and their self-esteem, not just in the setting, but long after they have left education and well into their adult life.

Dealing with such challenging behaviour can be extremely stressful and you may, at times, feel overwhelmed by some of the things you have seen and heard. But do not ever feel you are alone. Every TA (and teacher) has been through it at one time or another and you are not to blame. If you feel like you are to blame for the situation (and at times you will) it is important to speak to other colleagues about how you feel. In my current setting we are lucky enough to have a counsellor with whom we can speak if and when needed. However, if access to a trained professional is not available in your setting, it is crucial you speak to either the head teacher or your line manager (phase leader or year group leader) who will be able to arrange for you to speak to someone who will be able to support you through this difficult time.

Practical ideas

Have a 'behaviour book' in the classroom, where unacceptable behaviour can be logged, just in case the parent comes in to query what happened at any stage (as it has been known for a child to go home and tell parents the issue has not been dealt with fairly, or they have played no part in the incident).

Have a copy of the rules and sanctions up on the wall in the classroom, so the children can be reminded of them as and when needed. In addition to the rules and sanctions, the class rules or Classroom Charter need to be clearly displayed and referred to if the child is making the wrong choice.

Use a target card with a child who regularly uses unacceptable behaviour. This gives the child a visual reminder of how things are going (lesson by lesson). The setting can monitor the behaviour shown by the child throughout the day and also identify times in the day that seem to cause the child the most stress.

Talk to the child about what causes them to use unwanted behaviour in the setting (whether it is in response to a particular lesson, topic, member of staff or child).

Invite parents into the setting to talk about what triggers the unacceptable behaviour and which strategies are used to calm the child at home.

If there are core children who are regularly showing unacceptable behaviour, it may be necessary to speak to the phase leader, so an assembly around expectations and behaviour in the setting can be organised.

Tips

Tip 1: Make sure the rewards and sanctions set out in the behaviour policy are used consistently, so the child is clear about what they can do to earn these and which behaviours will result in them receiving a consequence.

Tip 2: Listen to both children when establishing what has occurred during an incident, especially if the children have made the wrong choice. By doing this, the children are far more likely to be honest with you. They will see that you are really interested in what went on and will not gain the impression that you have already made up your mind about who is the guilty party before you have even heard what they have to say (which would only make the children defensive and less likely to cooperate).

Tip 3: Be honest when talking to children about feelings and emotions. Show them that it is okay to be angry, and that it is a normal response when faced with something that makes them feel uncomfortable.

Tip 4: Set up an 'Anger Management Group' where children can explore their feelings in a safe and supportive environment. (See Chapter 5, which features more on strategies that can be used to support children to manage their emotions in a small-group situation.)

Tip 5: Model acceptable behaviour in and around the setting; use good manners, call people by their given name, do what is asked of you first time and be kind and helpful. Always set a good example. *But remember, you are only human.

Consistency

At the beginning of every academic year many new staff will join the primary setting 'family' in a variety of roles: teachers, TAs, dinner supervisors, cleaning staff and students; the list is never-ending. However, having so many new (and sometimes inexperienced) staff can sometimes cause issues with consistency. In a bid to overcome this, many primary schools now go through the main points of the behaviour policy annually (normally at the beginning of the school year), to ensure all new and existing staff are aware of which rewards and sanctions are available to them, and how they should be used consistently, to have the desired effect. At these meetings, staff will often be given the opportunity to share problems or issues they have experienced whilst trying to implement the policy or to discuss rewards and sanctions that may not be working as effectively as they once were. This can sometimes result in the document being re-worded or changed, so that common areas of confusion are explained more clearly.

Over the years, I have seen many examples of how unacceptable behaviour has been triggered by rewards, and sanctions being used inconsistently by staff (not out of malice, but due to them implementing strategies that they feel more confident using, as they may have used the strategy effectively in a previous setting or heard another colleague talking about a strategy that has worked well for them). Although these strategies may work in the short term, in the long term, the child will often become confused and use the very behaviour the behaviour policy was designed to prevent. Using the rewards and sanctions consistently will make sure that:

- The child has a clear understanding of what is expected of them in the setting from every member of staff they come into contact with.

- There can be no confusion about what is acceptable and what is not, as every member of staff is giving the same message.

- Children will not feel their behaviour has been dealt with differently or unfairly, as all members of staff will be using the same set of standards.

If it does become necessary to make changes to any aspect of the behaviour policy (for whatever reason), I would strongly suggest you are there when the children are told about them, as you will be able to answer questions about how these changes could affect them on a day-to-day basis. As a TA, you will play a vital role in reinforcing these changes, especially with children who struggle with change. It may be necessary to go through the changes multiple times, until the child gets used to them. You may also find you need to answer any questions from parents about the changes being made, as parents are often informed through letters that have been sent through the post (to ensure all parents receive the same message about expectation and behaviour in and around the setting).

Practical ideas

Have a copy of the rewards and sanctions on the wall in the classroom, so that you can refer to them as and when needed. *In the past, I have also sellotaped smaller versions of the rewards and sanctions to all of the desks, so there can be no confusion amongst the children regarding the rewards and sanctions used in the setting.

Keep a copy of the behaviour policy close at hand, so that you can refer to it should you need to check anything, especially when faced with a difficult situation for the first time; the child using a swear word or saying something that is totally inappropriate can sometimes be an issue that needs clarification.

Restraint

If a child is at risk of putting themselves or others in danger, then it may be necessary to remove the child from the classroom. As part of their training, in most schools, staff are now given some kind of restraint training. This is when external trainers come into the setting and work alongside staff to train them on the correct and safest way to restrain a child, if they should need to be removed from a situation. However, if your setting does not offer this, it may be necessary for you to ask for training, particularly if you feel you support a child who may need to be removed from the classroom, due to them regularly using unacceptable or dangerous behaviour. Restraint is always the last option and must be carefully considered before you make the decision to restrain (if there is time – but often there is not). It is important to exhaust all other options first (normally, your powers of persuasion will be enough to calm the situation down). However, once the decision has been made to restrain the child, and you (and the child) are safe, it is essential you fill in the relevant paperwork (usually called a 'restraint form'). The form will require you to record:

- The time and date the restraint took place.

- Where the restraint took place (in the classroom, in the playground or in another part of the setting).

- What the child was doing to warrant the restraint (in terms of behaviour: physical and verbal). *It is important to include as much detail as possible.

- Which staff witnessed the restraint.

- Which staff offered support or helped when you restrained the child.

- What course of action was taken as a result of the unacceptable behaviour – was the child given an in-house exclusion, fixed-term exclusion or permanent exclusion?

Practical ideas

Have a copy of the restraint policy and Team Teach procedures somewhere accessible, so that you can check on what needs to be recorded and how.

Produce an 'emergency red hand system' (a picture of a hand, backed on red paper, labelled with the class name) so that if an emergency arises, adult help and support is sent to the class immediately.

As an alternative to restraint, it may be possible to remove all of the other children from the classroom, leaving the child in class to calm down (and wait for parents to come, if they have been informed).

Tips

Tip 1: Stay calm and call for help from SMT as soon as it is safe to do so.

Tip 2: Use the 'red hand system' mentioned above, as it gets help to you as soon as possible.

Tip 3: Remind the children that they are not angry with you, and that you can help them deal with the situation if they just calm down.

If you are still reading this book and this chapter has not scared you off, you really are destined to be a TA. My intention throughout this book is to give you a true reflection of what it is like to be a TA. So there will be times when you witness a child doing or saying something that is totally inappropriate. But it is important to remember these incidents are a rare occurrence. It is also important to remember what a massive part you, as a TA, will play in teaching a child how to behave – how to become citizens of the future. When working with children, you will be teaching them to be adults who care for each other, respect each other and value differences.

Chapter 5
Small group working

Ever since the new curriculum was introduced in 2014, children needing additional support are no longer taken out of the classroom to work in small groups but are encouraged to stay in class and work in mixed-ability groups. It is thought that if children working below age-related expectations (below ARE) are supported by children who are more able, then both children benefit. The less able child will develop their knowledge and understanding of a subject, while the more able child will develop their questioning and reasoning skills.

In an ideal world, this strategy would be successful, and all children would work together and understand the task set. Unfortunately, we do not live in an ideal world, and there are many children who simply cannot access the curriculum. There are many different reasons for this. For example, the child might:

- have a special educational need or disability (SEND) issue
- speak English as an additional language (EAL)
- have a mild or severe learning difficulty
- have fallen behind their peers due to poor attendance, long-term illness or term-time holidays
- be experiencing an ongoing issue at home, which may affect the child's ability to concentrate on school work.

Therefore, as a TA, it may be necessary to organise small interventions that will support children with varying degrees of need. However, before these groups can be set up successfully, the specific needs of the children must be carefully considered. One way to do this is to read the SEN paperwork, as in the individual education plan (IEP) or individual teaching plan (ITP). By doing this, the work will be tailored to the specific needs of the child and will have a much more positive impact on the child and their future learning.

However, to write about all the different intervention groups that you may encounter in an average primary school would be impossible (as all settings use interventions differently). So I have decided to tell you about the most common groups I have been asked to run over the last 17 years.

Fine motor groups

Fine motor groups in my current setting have now become a daily occurrence, but the benefits far outweigh the amount of time and energy the group takes to set up and resource.

Encouraging the child to practise their fine motor skills and dexterity can have a positive impact not only on academic ability, but also on the ability to be more independent. Without these skills, the child may have difficulty carrying out some of the most important tasks needed to make progress in the setting: writing, using scissors and doing the small movements needed to tie up shoelaces and fasten up buttons and zips – just some of the skills that need to be mastered. Although there is not an instant 'cure' for fine motor difficulties, there is a range of interventions that can be used to develop these skills. However, before any groups take place, there are some things you first need to find out about the child:

- Is the child left- or right-handed?
- Which hand is most dominant (the hand the child tends to use for certain tasks)?
- Does the child have any SEND that hinders fine motor function?

Once it has become obvious which hand the child feels comfortable using, it may be necessary to approach the resource manager to ask if resources can be purchased to support the child with developing fine motor function. There is now a wide range of left- and right-handed equipment available to support children who are having fine motor difficulties. However, before any purchases are made I suggest meeting up with the SENDCo, who can tell you what resources are already available in the setting (as they may be being used to support another child in the setting). The most common resources that must be made available to the child in every single lesson include:

- rulers
- scissors
- computer mouse
- pencils
- pens
- a writing wedge (to ensure the book or paper is positioned at the right angle to make writing more comfortable)
- a seating wedge (so the child is able to reach the table and has the correct posture needed to write).

As the child gets used to the new equipment, it is crucial that the child is observed a number of times, to determine whether the equipment is age-appropriate and meets the needs of the child.

Cutting

Cutting can also be problematic for some children, and during any given day you may come across children who find it extremely difficult to use a pair of scissors, regardless of which year group you support (from a cut-and-stick activity in Reception, to cutting around their work in Year 6). Children who struggle to use a pair of scissors can get extremely frustrated, but if patience and cutting skills are modelled to the child, the child will soon start to show improvements. As with all skills, the child needs practice, practice and more practice. However, with perseverance, the child can succeed. These are just some of the ways cutting skills can be improved:

Tips

Tip 1: Show the child how to use a use a pair of scissors (it is a skill). The child will need to learn how to: move the paper around; use small and fluent movements to cut out their work; and take their time.

Tip 2: Have left- and right-handed scissors available for the child, in order for them to decide which feels most comfortable when carrying out a particular task. *I am left-handed, but cannot for the life of me cut with left-handed scissors; right-handed scissors feel far more comfortable for cutting.

Tip 3: Provide children with specialised scissors, to see which pair suits them. There are now many different types of scissors available to support children with fine motor difficulties – either scissors where there are two sets of finger holes (so the teacher or the TA can guide the child whilst using the scissors) or scissors that have a spring attached to the handles (which encourages the child to use their whole hand and does not require the child to use the pincer movement at all).

Tip 4: Invite parents into the setting, to work alongside their child during the cutting skills intervention. By doing this, the child will be more likely to be encouraged to practise these skills at home (especially if they are given lots of practical ideas to try).

Practical ideas

I know it sounds silly, but it important that all interventions, even 'cutting skills', are put on the timetable, to make sure the provision the child receives is easy to track (essential if the child has or is in the process of being assessed for an ECHP).

Produce a sheet with different lines and patterns on it, which will encourage the child to practise all of the skills that have been taught, e.g. making small, considered movements and turning the paper instead of turning their hand. As the child grows in confidence, so can the difficulty of the lines; you can change the direction of the lines and the shape of the lines (wavy and zig-zag lines are a great way to develop cutting skills).

Make sure you speak to the resource manager about the types of resources that are now available to support children with fine motor difficulties. At present there are a wide range of books and IT-based resources available in SEND catalogues, but a decision must be made about which best meet the needs of the child.

Use activities where children are encouraged to use tweezers to pick up and move small items such as pompoms, dry pasta and buttons, which allows them to practise the pincer movement.

Letter formation

Many children struggle with letter formation, whether they are in Early Years or in Year 6. To find out how best to support letter formation within the setting, I recommend you read the handwriting policy. In the policy, there will be clear guidance on what the child is expected to know and at what age the child should have mastered these skills. There is a range of strategies that you can use in the classroom to support all children with letter formation:

- Show the children how to hold the pen or pencil properly; model the correct pencil grip at the start of every lesson.

- Make sure the child is sitting on the chair properly, with all six legs on the floor (the four legs of the chair and their two legs), and tucked in enough to support the correct posture.

- Encourage the child to sit up when writing (not to slouch) and use their other hand to support the book, which will stop the book moving around when they are trying to write. *You could find and display an image from the Internet to show children the correct way to sit when writing.

- Model the correct way to form letters; where the start and end of each letter is; and whether they are ascenders or descenders (ascenders sit on the line – a, b and c – whereas descenders go below the line: p, j, q and g). A good way I have found to support a child having difficulty with these letters is to put a green dot where the letter should start and a red dot where it ends. As the child gets more confident, the dots can be removed.

However, there may be some children who get so stressed at the very thought of completing any type of writing activity that you may be asked to offer more individualised support. If this is the case, it is possible you may be asked to organise a small intervention group to help children who have difficulty forming letters correctly. In this group, you will need to use a range of strategies that provide children with the opportunity to practise the skills needed to improve letter formation, in a less formal way. However, before you set up the group I suggest you find out whether the child is left- or right-handed and what the child actually has difficulty with. By doing this, you will be able to quickly assess which strategies may help and support the child to improve their letter formation (as left- and right-handed learners can form letters differently). It is now possible to purchase letter-formation books that have been produced to support both left- and right-handed learners. Children who are trying to join their writing will have difficulty if not shown the right way for them. This is why it is so important to determine which hand the child writes with. At a very young age, the child may still be deciding which hand feels most comfortable; this is why it is so important to provide both left- and right-handed equipment (it may change depending on what activity the child is doing). Strategies that you may find helpful when supporting a child who is finding letter formation difficult include:

Tips

Tip 1: Have a range of pens and pencils available to the children so the child can choose which one feels the most comfortable; there are now triangular versions of both, which encourage the child to use the correct pencil grip.

Tip 2: Make sure you have left- and right-handed resources available, as some children will change the hand they use, depending on what is being asked of them. *I have worked with some children who are 'left-handed', but cannot use a ruler that has been specifically designed to support left-handed learners; I have also supported children who swap hands constantly as they complete a writing task.

Tip 3: Use patterns (wavy lines, zig-zags and circles) to encourage the child to practise the skills needed for more formal letter formation.

Tip 4: Give the child a shape with a thicker line around it, so they can practise writing over this shape and moving their hands in different directions.

Tip 5: Encourage the children to make shapes in sand trays, out of homemade play dough, or with their finger in the air, on the carpet in front of them or on their friend's back (as their friends can tell them if they have formed it correctly).

Practical ideas

Have a wide range of mark-making resources available, as this gives the child the opportunity to choose which media they feel most confident using; chalk, chunky pens, felt-tip pens and paint are just some of the resources that are widely available in any primary setting.

Provide the children who are having difficulty with letter formation with a pencil grip, so they can practise how to hold the pencil properly.

Make a set of upper and lower case letters using different textures: sandpaper, cotton wool, felt, wood, hessian and any other texture that allows the child to feel what it is like to make the letter.

Give the children incentives (not bribes!) to encourage them to practise letter formation; handwriting certificates can be an incredibly effective way to reward a child who has mastered a new skill.

Present children with special handwriting pens in a celebration assembly as a reward for making a real effort with letter formation. (Invite parents, carers or friends of the family.) The impact of these assemblies can be massive, not just on their academic work but also on their attitude to learning.

However, there may come a time when you have used every strategy you can think of with a particular child, and they are still not making the expected progress. At this point, it may be necessary to speak to the SENDCo, to determine what provision has been made for the child previously and what could be offered in the future. If all areas of support from within the setting have been exhausted, it may be necessary to make a referral to an outside agency (more than likely, an occupational therapist). When the therapists come into the setting initially, you may be asked to provide them with some information about the child: whether the child is left- or right-handed, tasks the child finds difficult, which strategies have been used and how successful they have been. Once the therapist has the full picture of the child and the difficulties they experience with letter formation, they will then be able to offer advice and resources that will be tailored to their need. In some settings, therapists often work alongside TAs to 'teach' them specially designed programmes, to make sure the child receives support every day. Although this can seem like a daunting prospect, the skills you will learn can be used with many other children in a wide variety of situations (and it will not do you any harm to add this to your CV).

Tying shoelaces, using zips and doing/undoing buttons

It sounds silly, but some tasks, such as tying shoelaces, using zips and undoing/doing up buttons, are skills that need to be mastered by children in the setting as soon as possible. If the child is unable to do these tasks in the setting, it can cause them to become stressed and anxious when being asked to get changed before and after a PE session, get ready for swimming lessons, tie their laces and zip their coats up for playtimes and dinnertimes (it can also be a source of stress for you, when you have to dress 30 children at the beginning and end of every PE session). Although these difficulties are to be expected at an early age (especially in Early Years and KS1), there will also be those children who are further up the school (in upper KS1 and KS2) who are unable to do these tasks due to a lack of fine motor skills. Often, it will be you who notices the child is having a difficulty, as it may be part of your role to supervise the children when they are changing for PE or swimming sessions. It may also be you who spots a child struggling to tie their shoelaces in the corridor as you move around the setting.

But you can help the child overcome these difficulties (using the growing number of skills you will have in your TA 'toolkit'). You may sit with the child whom you noticed in the corridor and show them how to tie their shoelaces (spending some time practising, until the child is able to do it independently). But, more often than not, you will be asked to organise a group that focuses on the self-help tasks a child needs to do independently. There are many quick and simple activities I have used over the years to help develop and strengthen the muscles in the child's hand. I hope you find them useful:

Tips

Tip 1: Have a variety of buttons sewn onto a blanket and encourage the child to put them through the button holes you have made on the other side of the blanket.

Tip 2: Provide the children with a pair of shoes with shoelaces in them; show the children how to do up the laces step by step. *It may be necessary to provide a visual step-by-step guide to support the children, which could also be sent home for the child to practise with the help and support of parents.

Tip 3: Give the children a pair of tweezers and get them to move small buttons and marbles from one plate to another, which will again allow them to develop the muscles in their thumb and forefinger. Again, turning this into a competition can do wonders for the child's confidence: who can move the most marbles? Which child can pick up the most buttons?

Tip 4: Provide the children with pegs and a paper plate, to give them the opportunity to practise their pincer movement.

Tip 5: Produce a 'fine motor booklet' that can be sent home so the parent can encourage the child to practise fine motor skills at home.

Tip 6: Practise getting changed and unchanged; to help with this, each child could be given an A3 sheet of paper with their name on. The sheet would have a set of footprints on it (for the child to place their shoes on) and a square (to put their clothes on). *This strategy can also be used to support a child with autism, as they often have difficulty organising themselves.

Practical ideas

Activity	Benefits to the child	Resources
Threading	Develops the pincer movement needed (the thumb and forefinger being used to grip objects) and hand–eye coordination	Pipe cleaners, string, buttons, pasta, beads (in a variety of sizes) and spaghetti (not cooked, obviously!)
Posting money into a money box	Gives the child an opportunity to practise manipulating coins in their hand; hand–eye coordination; pincer movement	Pretend coins and money box
Making home-made play dough	Action of kneading play dough helps develop the muscles needed to carry out fine motor tasks	Home-made play dough recipe: flour, salt, cream of tartar, oil, food colouring, glycerin, mixing bowl and wooden spoon

Activity	Benefits to the child	Resources
Gluing and sticking	Offers opportunity to practise cutting out accurately; hand–eye coordination; pincer grip	Glue, scissors and pictures that will interest the child: fairies, patterns, cartoon characters and old magazines to cut up
Sewing	Hand–eye coordination and pincer grip	Needles in a variety of sizes, string or cotton of different thickness, material in many thicknesses
Making sandwiches	Hand–eye coordination and pincer grip	Bread, butter and sandwich fillings (although you will need to consider any children with an allergy and send a letter home telling the parents, before the child takes part in any food-based activities)

Throughout the school day there may be small pockets of time when a child has the opportunity to spend a couple of minutes doing an activity that will help them develop their fine motor skills. Therefore, you may wish to talk to the teacher, to see if it is possible to set up a fine motor area in the classroom, so the area is always accessible to the children. The area could have the following activities available:

Tips

Tip 1: Have a box of fine motor activities that can be accessed if and when the child has some free-time, or as a reward for finishing work; fiddle toys, stress balls and threading are just some of the activities that could be made available.

Tip 2: Provide the children with Mehndi-type designs, as the patterns are normally quite intricate, which will not only develop their fine motor skills, but also their patience and dexterity.

If you are inexperienced or have received no specific training on the topic of fine motor difficulties, the thought of being asked to support an individual or small group can be unnerving, to say the least. If this is part of your role, it may be necessary to attend a training course to enhance your skills and knowledge around the difficulties faced by children who have fine motor difficulties. But you do not need to worry; any training needed will be arranged by the setting and form part of your continued professional development (CPD). Failing this, it may be possible to shadow a more experienced TA, who will share a variety of well-tested strategies that could be used to support children you may be asked to work with. Whichever route is taken, you will gain an in-depth knowledge of what fine motor difficulties are and the effect they can have on the child (not just on academic ability, but also on the child's confidence) and also an understanding of which possible approaches would best meet the needs of the child.

Gross motor skills

At times, colleagues in the setting will talk about 'gross motor issues' or 'gross motor groups'. The term 'gross motor difficulties' means difficulties with controlling and coordinating limbs. In the setting, a child with gross motor problems will often find it difficult to move around the setting without bumping into other children or objects in the setting (such as chairs and tables). Such a child may have difficulty working out where their bodies are in relation to others. Although it would be lovely if we could fix all these difficulties at the click of our fingers, unfortunately for these children, there is no quick fix.

However, children can be taught how to develop gross motor function and use their limbs in a more coordinated way. This is where your amazing skills come in again. Once again, you may be asked to support an individual child who is experiencing gross motor issues or set up a 'gross motor group', which could support a small group of children (normally no more than six children) to develop their gross motor movements. In order for these groups to be successful, you may need to attend a training course (similar to fine motor training), which will provide some background on what gross motor skills are, how difficulties with these can affect the child and what strategies can be used to help a child overcome them. Some of the most important gross motor skills a child needs to master are:

- balancing when standing still and when moving around (sometimes called 'static' and 'dynamic' balance)
- hand–eye coordination
- inner core strength and stability.

In order to give the child the opportunity to develop these skills in a fun and exciting way, the following activities could be used.

Activities that develop hand–eye coordination

- throwing and catching games
- hitting a moving target
- bouncing a ball on the floor or on a racket
- throwing a ball or bean bag at a target
- introducing the child to racket sports; tennis and badminton can be used to develop gross motor function (especially if balls of different shapes and sizes are used)
- providing the child with the opportunity to play team sports; football, basketball and rounders are particularly effective
- hitting a ball from a stand, where the ball stands on top and the child hits it from a static position.

Activities that develop balance ('static' or 'dynamic') and core stability

- standing on a PE spot with both feet on the floor (these are usually used to mark out a safe area for PE sessions)
- hopping from one leg to the other
- balancing on one leg and then swapping to the other

- getting down on all fours and lifting one leg off the floor, then the other (it is also beneficial to lift one arm off the floor, and then the other arm)
- skipping
- running in different directions
- stopping safely after running
- gymnastic exercises
- encouraging children to travel across a bench (either walking forwards or backwards across it, or sliding across it on their stomach)
- setting up an obstacle course that is made from objects found in many primary settings: benches to walk and slide across; PE mats, which can be rolled across or crawled across; and a 'parachute', which can be crawled under.

Practising these skills in small groups or individually can have a massive impact on the child and their self-esteem. As the child grows in confidence, the child will start to feel like part of the class to such an extent that they will feel comfortable enough to join in games alongside their peers.

Tips

Tip 1: Have a PE Star of the Week certificate, which can be given to the child who has made the most progress with skills, attitude and sportsmanship.

Tip 2: Give out stickers to children who have made progress within the lesson: encouraging others, thinking of a different way of doing a task or being a good team player are just some of the ways a child can impress.

Tip 3: Ask the child to 'show off' their new-found skills to the class, a small group of friends or members of staff the child feels comfortable with (e.g. dinner supervisors, TAs from previous classes and the head teacher).

Practical ideas

Organise an inter-class football or basketball match to encourage the child to practise their gross motor skills in a safe and controlled environment.

Make the child 'team captain' from time to time; this will make the other children in the class see the child's other qualities, rather than the difficulties they have.

Talk to the child about which activities cause the most stress, which skills they would really like to master, and what might need to happen for them to achieve this.

If, after all of these interventions have been carried out, the child is still having difficulty with their gross motor movements, it may be necessary to contact the SENDCo. At this point, they will only be able to offer advice and support on which strategies could support the child further. However, if it gets to a point where all of these strategies have been used and the child is still struggling, the SENDCo may need to make a referral to an outside agency (either to an occupational therapist or a physiotherapist). Both of these professionals will be able to offer practical ideas and advice and recommend a range of resources that could be purchased to support future interventions with the child. In a similar way to fine motor groups, the therapist may work alongside the member of staff who supports the child with gross motor function (usually the TA) and go through a specially-written programme that can be reused to support other children in the setting who have gross motor difficulties.

Children can experience difficulties with gross motor movements for a variety of reasons (all of which need to be considered when the finer details of the group are discussed with the class teacher and SENDCo). Common factors that may affect the development of gross motor function include:

- a pre-existing medical condition that affects gross motor function (e.g. dyspraxia)
- the child having a physical disability (e.g. spina bifida, cerebral palsy) or being wheelchair-bound
- long-term illness
- developmental delay.

At times, you may not notice a huge improvement in the child's gross motor function, but if you think about the movement the child had before taking part in the group, I guarantee the child will have made a massive improvement. I know that time is precious, but it is sometimes important to reflect on the children you have worked with and the progress they have made. After all, it is one of the many reasons you do the job.

Social interaction groups (SIG)/ friendship groups

For some children, school is a positive environment where they have the opportunity to be with their friends, interact with adults and peers and have fun (as well as learn, obviously). However, for some children (and some adults) school can be a horrible place, which causes them to feel an immense amount of pressure and stress – pressure to do well, pressure to have the most friends and stress when they feel they cannot achieve this. Although there could be many reasons for this, I have found that some children simply lack the social skills needed to be able to manage these situations successfully. But what *are* social skills, I hear you ask. Social skills allow the child to interact with others (through verbal and non-verbal ways – body language and facial expressions): to make friends, to negotiate, to resolve conflict and to express thoughts and feelings. So, being the social butterfly that you are, who else could they ask to run a social skills group?

At this point it would be good to speak to the SENDCo, who will be able to offer some advice on practical activities that could be used to develop social skills (whatever the need of the child). As you get to know the children, you will soon get a feel for what a child excels at and what they struggle with, which can be invaluable when deciding which activities to use with the group. Some medical conditions that need to be taken into consideration include:

- **Autism:** A child with a diagnosis of autism often has issues around some aspects of social interaction, especially when having a conversation about a topic they are passionate about; the child will often talk *at* the other child rather than *to* them. *If this happens too often, the other children may start to avoid the child and start to brand the child as 'strange' or 'weird'.

- **ADHD:** A child with ADHD can sometimes shout out comments that are inappropriate or offend others. Such behaviour can make maintaining a friendship difficult, as the peers may see the child as 'naughty' and may not want to interact with them, as they might 'get them into trouble'.

- **Speech and language difficulties:** A child with a speech and language difficulty can struggle with a wide variety of tasks. One of these is definitely to talk to their peers and make themselves understood. Due to these difficulties, the child may withdraw from the group, which may isolate the child from the rest of their class.

But if the child is supported by an understanding and supportive person (you!) then great progress can be made. Sometimes, the progress made by the child may not be so obvious to you, as you spend a lot of time with the child. But other members of staff who do not see the child that often will sometimes comment on the difference in the child. It is important to relay this compliment back to the child, as it can have a massive impact on them, boosting their confidence and spurring them on to try even harder than they already were.

See below for a wide range of activities that can be used to support children who have difficulties interacting with others. I hope you will try some of them with the children you may be asked to support.

Tips

Tip 1: Set up a friendship group or Social Interaction Group (SIG) with the child and other children who are good role models and make friends easily. During the session (and all of the fun activities you have devised) the child will soon start to pick up what a good friend is and the qualities that can make a good friend: someone who listens, cares, is kind, supportive and honest, and always there for you, no matter what. *If the group is supportive, the child is far more likely to try new skills and experiment with them, as they feel safe and able to take risks.

Tip 2: Teach negotiation skills through board games (which can be used in the class as well as in groups). These games can teach the children so many skills that will help them socially: e.g. turn taking, negotiating, asking for help, working together and learning to lose (a very important skill to learn).

Tip 3: Talk to children about strategies that could be used if an issue arises through role play.

Tip 4: Make sure you talk about peer pressure and how this can be used to pressure somebody into doing something that is either wrong or that they do not feel comfortable doing.

Tip 5: Give the child a mirror during group sessions, so they can look at their own facial expressions. This strategy will make the child more aware of what messages they are giving out to others.

Tip 6: Set up a 'buddy system' so the child has someone to play with at playtime and dinnertimes and ask questions of if they are unsure of anything. *Remember to tell the 'buddy' to feed back to the teacher if the child is worried or anxious about anything, so it can be dealt with immediately.

Tip 7: Put the children into 'talk partners' in lessons where they may need to discuss a topic. By doing this, the child will have someone there to support them when offering an answer or opinion.

Tip 8: Use role play so the child can practise how to negotiate or initiate a conversation. *If possible, use scenario cards, so the child can pick the situation that they feel most comfortable acting out with a partner:

You are going to the **shop**	to get **a bag of candy floss.**
hairdressers	**a chocolate bar.**
fair	**a haircut.**

Practical ideas

Make a set of scenario cards to introduce difficult topics of discussion to the class. Ask children to imagine how they would feel coming into the setting if other children did not make them feel welcome, or excluded them from team games. It may also be necessary to ask the children what could be done to make the new child feel like part of the class.

Send the child to another class to give a message to a member of staff they know well. Pre-warn the teacher, so the child gets a positive welcome (this does not always happen if a child interrupts a lesson).

Set up a speech and language table, with pictures and objects that may be used to stimulate children to talk together; circus animals, zoo animals, shopping, playground and leaves are just some of the pictures and objects that can give child the opportunity to tell others about a visit they have been on, or about an up-and-coming event. *It may help to encourage the child to bring objects from home that they may want to talk about.

If these skills are not developed, the child will struggle in the setting, feeling isolated and as though they are not part of the class. Having these feelings can have a devastating effect on the child, not just on their self-confidence, but also on their ability to get involved in their learning. They may be frightened of ridicule.

If the child is still struggling, despite all of the interventions that have been put in place, it is essential that the SENDCo becomes involved. The SENDCo may be able to offer new strategies. However, if these are not successful and the child is still having problems interacting with other children, the decision to make a referral to an outside agency may be made (speech and language therapist (SALT) or a play therapist). When the SALT visits for the first time, you will be asked to provide them with any background information that may be relevant: what aspects of social skills the child has an issue with, what inventions have been used and any medical issues that could affect social interaction. The therapist will then carry out an assessment on the speech and language ability of the child. Once the therapist has a full picture of the difficulties the child experiences, they will be able to offer advice and a range of resources that have been designed to best meet the needs of the child. As a result of this, the therapist may also work alongside the TA to teach them how to implement the specially-designed programme of activities daily, which will of course have a massive impact on the progress made by the child. The therapist will monitor the progress made by the child (normally every term) so changes can be made to the programme in response to the needs of the child.

Pre-tutoring

Although pre-tutoring is not a specific group, it may still be necessary to work with an individual child or small group to explain some of the more topic-specific words the children will hear during lessons in the setting. The language used in a primary school can often be confusing and, if not understood, can cause the child to feel anxious about getting into trouble for not understanding what is being asked of them. However, the child must be taken out of the classroom before the lesson starts, so they have some understanding of the vocabulary and concepts that will be included in a lesson later on in the day. Exposing the child to vocabulary that will feature in subsequent lessons can have a massive impact on their ability to understand and participate in the lesson (especially if the child speaks EAL or has a language delay, developmental delay or cognition and learning difficulties). At times, during the sessions, it may also be possible to make cross-curricular links between lessons, to provide the child with the opportunity to make connections between areas of learning and previous experiences they have had. This will also give the child a chance to see the topics from different viewpoints, which can develop their thinking (their questioning and reasoning skills in particular). Encouraging the children in such a small group can help the child build on previous knowledge and grow in confidence until they start to become an independent learner, able to complete a task totally unsupported. However, it is important to remember that the support a child may need may change from lesson to lesson, depending on the level of understanding the child has in a particular topic (some children may excel in some areas, but struggle in others).

Practical ideas

Meet the teacher daily, to discuss which key vocabulary needs to be introduced to the child and when on the timetable this can happen (to have the most impact).

Prepare a practical activity, which could be used to explain a concept or vocabulary the child finds confusing. Role play is always a good way to introduce the child to language that is unfamiliar.

Have vocabulary cards on each desk, to which the children can refer throughout the lesson if they need to remind themselves what the words and phrases mean.

Tips

Tip 1: Introduce the child to as much English as possible (taking into consideration the ability and needs of the child). But it may be necessary to revert back to their home language if you have the facilities to do so; parents, a translator or another child who speaks the same language as the child can all be called upon, if necessary.

Tip 2: Provide the child with pictures to accompany words if possible. Visual clues are a great way to develop understanding.

Tip 3: Have key vocabulary on the wall around the classroom, so the child can refer to this as and when needed.

As the child develops their understanding of the English language, it may be necessary to pre-tutor the child less. However, it is still important to keep a close eye on the child, to ensure they still understand what is being asked of them, and to know when to reintroduce any necessary pre-tutoring.

Maths support (formerly numeracy)

I have to admit that maths is not my favourite subject, and now that the curriculum has changed dramatically, I find it even more difficult to get excited about maths. In terms of both content and expectation of each year group (in my opinion both have increased dramatically) I have found it more challenging to determine whether a child is working below the level expected, at the expected level or working at greater depth. However, now that the curriculum has moved away from giving a child a level, the responsibility for delivering lessons and assessing children has been firmly placed back with the teacher.

However, in the new 'Mastery Maths Curriculum', the TA plays a crucial role, by working alongside children who need additional support to extend their knowledge in a more practical way. The mastery approach encourages children to explore the use of number through the questions the teacher and TA ask. Challenging children and getting them to think of many ways a particular question can be answered can encourage them to think of all the different possibilities (to think outside the box), which will give them a deeper understanding of the topic. To write about every single aspect of the new mastery curriculum would be impossible, so I have decided to include a range of activities that can be used to support the most common areas of maths. I hope you are able to use some of these:

My answer is 56. What could the question be?

Now lots of children will put answers such as:

50 + 6 =
55 + 1=
57 – 1 =

and all the other associated number facts. However, some children may write the answer as a word problem:

If I have 50 and add 6, what number have I got?

What is one more than 55?

If the child has reached a conclusion by themselves, they are far more likely to retain the information and, as they grow in confidence, will start to make links between other areas of maths.

One of the most important parts of the mastery curriculum for a TA is the way children are now expected to explore maths topics; there is now a far more hands-on approach to maths. Under the new curriculum, you may hear a teacher say they are going to use the concrete, pictorial and abstract (CPA) strategy to introduce a new maths topic:

- **Concrete:** Initially, the teacher or TA will model how to use concrete apparatus (counters, compare bears, Uni-link, blocks and Numicon, to name but a few) to work out a number equation (or calculation).

- **Pictorial:** After the child has had the opportunity to practise using concrete apparatus, the child will be shown how to represent what they have done using dots, flowers, cars or any other picture the child feels comfortable drawing.

- **Abstract:** In this stage, the concrete apparatus is removed and the child is introduced to the mathematical symbols that are to be used to replace the pictures the child used to represent their thinking. When the children have reached this stage of understanding, they will be expected to work out maths problems 'in their heads' without the need to use any practical or written methods.

Going through these stages gives the child a greater opportunity to explore and develop a deeper understanding of the topic and become a mathematical 'whizz'.

Arithmetic

Number is a funny topic, as children often think they do not need to know it. If I had a pound each time a child has asked me how and when they will use number skills in their life, then I would definitely be lying on a beach somewhere exotic. I have had to explain on numerous occasions how important it is to master these skills, as they will need to use number in every aspect of daily life:

- **Banking:** has the right money been paid into the bank (overtime/ correct hourly rate)?

- **Budgeting:** how many treats can you afford, as well as the rent and bills (and is there enough left over to save)?

- **Wages:** does the money paid reflect the number of hours worked?

- **Shopping:** can you afford to pay for items; will you save money if you buy multipacks or buy in bulk?

- **Home:** can you measure an area that needs to be painted, carpeted or fenced?

- **Travel:** can you work out exchange rates (will an item cost more when bought in the UK, or is better to buy the item whilst abroad)?

Tips

Tip 1: Link as many activities to real-life situations as possible, so children realise how important maths is (without lecturing them).

Tip 2: Use lots of practical activities; Numicon (which is now being used in many primary schools across the country), counters, Base 10, Unifix cubes, fraction bars, place value cards, 10 frames and counters will all help the children understand the concept of number (whichever operation is being used: addition, subtraction, multiplication or division).

Tip 3: Introduce the children to place value charts as soon as possible, to check the child knows what the value of each number is. *Make sure you remind the children about the units column now being called the 'ones' column. (I still have not entirely got my head around it; I still make the occasional slip, but the children are quick to correct me.)

Tip 4: Use bead strings to introduce number bonds to 10 and 100.

Tip 5: Have a large set of numbers from 0–100; these can be used to practise ordering numbers.

Tip 6: Do some kind of basic addition and multiplication task daily, so the child is able to recall the number facts quickly, as and when needed. Quick recall is essential for the many different tests the children are expected to do. *Start off by doing them in some sort of order: $1 \times 2 = ?$, $2 \times 2 = ?$; and then move onto mixed-up questions: $12 \times 2 = ?$, $2 \times 2 = ?$. The same strategy can be used for number bonds: $0 + 10 = ?$, $1 + 9 = ?$, $2 + 8 = ?$; and then once the child becomes confident give the same calculations in a different order: $10 + 0 = ?$, $5 + 5 = ?$, $9 + 1 = ?$. *A great time to practise these skills (as well as in the lesson) is when the child is lining up for dinner, or whenever there are a few spare minutes in the day!

Tip 7: Bingo games can encourage children to think about: the properties of shape; the total of two numbers being added; the difference between numbers; and quick recall of multiplication facts, to name but a few things.

Tip 8: Use visual methods to represent different concepts; use birthday cakes or pizzas when first introducing the children to fractions.

Tip 9: The Singapore bar method (which is recommended in the maths curriculum) can be used to teach children to think about what an amount, a fraction or the difference between two amounts 'looks like' as a part of a whole (something children often struggle with).

Tip 10: Introduce the children to '10 frames', where each square represents tens instead of ones, which can encourage children to work out calculations using bigger numbers.

Funny story

I once had the pleasure of observing a teacher with a really strong Irish accent teaching maths to a small group of children with SEND issues. I will never forget the teacher asking a child what he would get if he added together a three and a three. (At this point, I feel I need to let you know the number three is pronounced 'tree' in a strong Irish accent.) In response to the question the child stood up, pushed his chest out and shouted, 'Two trees, Miss!' The teacher looked at me and quickly realised the children in Birmingham did not quite understand the accent. *The children still remember the lesson and the teaching behind it, even though it happened nearly five years ago.

Measurement and geometry (formerly shape, space and measure)

The topic of measures and geometry is a massive area of maths, which covers many different topics. Again, to write about every single one would simply take too long, so I have decided to write about the activities you, as a TA, may use in order to give the child the opportunity to deepen their knowledge in this area of maths:

Activities that support the teaching of capacity

- Introduce Early Years children to the topic of capacity through play, as they can experiment with using different-sized containers. You could even set the children small challenges: how many of the smaller containers will it take to fill the big container? You could even encourage the children to estimate (an educated guess, not just the first number that comes into their head) how many containers it may take.

- Use measuring jugs and different containers with younger children, so children can learn the concepts of 'more than' and 'less than'. Older children could use jugs to determine which container can hold more and justify why they have reached this conclusion.

- Encourage children to transfer liquid from one container to another. *Add glitter to liquid, which will help to engage even the most reluctant learner.

- Introduce units of measurement when measuring capacity from a very early age: millilitres, litres and gallons, cubic inches and cubic metres, to name but a few.

Practical ideas

Put up posters around the classroom about capacity, including the vocabulary that children need to use and the equipment that can be used to measure it.

Produce a small vocabulary card, which the children can keep on their desks to refer to during the lesson for when they forget which mathematical words they may need to include in their work.

Activities that support the teaching of mass/ weight

- In the early stages of learning about weight, a child could be encouraged to hold objects in their hand to see which objects feel lighter or heavier. This will allow the children to start making comparisons from the earliest opportunity, using mathematical vocabulary such as lighter, heavier, more than and less than.

- Have a set of scales in the classroom, where children are encouraged to weigh themselves and other objects around the classroom (see the practical ideas underneath with suggestions on which objects around the setting can be weighed). From my experience, children get excited at the prospect of using scales (whether balance scales or those used for weighing).

- Introduce the children to the units of measurement that represent the weight of an object (appropriate to the age and ability of the child). Grams and kilograms are usually introduced quite early on, so the children have a good understanding of the words associated with the topic.

Practical ideas

Have a weight table, with many objects the child may like to weigh: fruit, teddy bear, toy car and beads, and the actual weights too. (One of the children I worked with in the past used to love checking the weight of the standard 'compare bear' weights; he also used to check the sand-timers, to see whether they really did last for one, two and five minutes.)

To encourage older children to investigate weight and mass, you could produce challenge cards, with questions such as: Which object on the table do you think is the heaviest? What is the difference between the weight of the teddy bear and the weight of the toy car?

Put up posters around the classroom with the vocabulary children need to know about weight/mass.

Produce a small vocabulary card for the children, which they can keep on their desks so they can refer to them if they forget the mathematical word they may need to use in their work.

Activities that support the teaching of length

- Have a variety of measuring instruments available when measuring the length of an object, so the child has to make a decision about which resource would be most appropriate. In most primary settings, the children would have access to a ruler, a measuring tape, a tape measure and a trundle wheel. *But it would take a long time to measure the playground using a ruler, and it isn't easy to measure the width of the corridor using a trundle wheel. So children need to be able to think about which piece of equipment would be most appropriate in each situation.

- Introduce the children to the correct unit of measurement as soon as possible: millimetres, centimetres, metres, miles and kilometres. (You can also measure in feet and inches.)

Practical ideas

Put up posters around the classroom with the vocabulary children need to know about length.

Produce a small vocabulary card for the children to keep on their desks so they can refer to them if they forget the mathematical word they may need to use.

Have a measuring table in the classroom so children can measure the length, width and the circumference of objects (depending on their age and ability). Objects such as a football, a ruler (and before you say 30 cm, remember it has the edges as well, so it is slightly longer), a book, a car and a teddy bear are just some of the objects that you may want to try with the children you support.

Link measuring where possible to real-life situations, so children can see why they need to know how to measure accurately – to work out the area of a room for carpets and painting, or the perimeter of a garden for buying or making a fence.

Make the lessons interactive and fun!

Shape

As the name suggests, a large part of the mastery curriculum is being able to name the most common two-dimensional (2D) and three-dimensional (3D) shapes and their properties. Activities that can be used to reinforce this include:

- Jigsaws.
- Shape dominoes.
- Matching the shape to the initial letter sound.
- Matching shapes to their properties.
- Playing a 'guess the shape game' where the child reads out clues and the rest of the group has to guess which shape the child is trying to describe. The shapes could also be put in a 'feely bag' so the child can feel the shape and give clues to the rest of the group, so they can guess which shape the child is trying to describe.
- Placing a sticky note on the forehead of a child (on the sticky you can write the name of the shape). The child then has to guess which shape they have been given by asking the rest of the group 'yes' or 'no' questions, to determine the shape.
- Making shapes using nets will help the child to see how nets are used to make 3D shapes. *This will help the child visualise the faces and vertices of the shape.
- Having a variety of maths posters around the setting, so the children can refer to them as and when needed (with 2D shape, 3D shape, and the properties).

Once the child is confident with the properties of 2D and 3D shapes, they will start to explore shape, either physically or by visualising the shape. This will encourage some children to start making links between other areas of maths. For instance, some children may begin to think about how some shapes fit together perfectly without any gaps (tesselation), whilst others will begin to think about the properties of more complex shapes. So what is thought to be 'a small activity' to extend learning can actually become an opportunity for the child to carry out some independent research (at home, maybe).

English (formerly literacy)

Since the new SATs were brought in last year (2016) I have seen the expectations in writing rise dramatically for teacher, children and support staff alike. The pressure to do well in English has now reached new heights and, as with all subjects, there will be some children who excel in English, as well as those who struggle. However, whatever ability the child has, English sessions are now made up of three different elements:

- writing
- spelling, punctuation and grammar (SPaG)
- speaking and listening (S and L).

Reading (see p. 145) is also a part of the English National Curriculum. Some schools include it within the main teaching of English, while others teach it discretely. Whilst some children may find one particular area of English difficult, others may struggle with all three areas. So, before any groups are formed, it is important to sit down with the class teacher to discuss which children will benefit from the support a small group can give.

Over an academic year, children are now expected to practise writing in many different genres, and by the time they are ready to leave the setting (in Year 6), they must be competent at writing:

- non-chronological reports
- chronological reports

- recounts
- letters
- invitations
- lists
- instructional text
- persuasive letters
- narrative.

Although the teacher will still give the main input to children, it may be necessary to reword or model some of what the teacher has said, so children can carry out the task that has been set successfully (albeit at a slightly slower pace).

Practical ideas

Have posters up around the classroom with positive words and phrases, so the group knows what is needed to make a positive learning environment. As I have said many times before, if the child feels happy and safe, they are more likely to take risks with their ideas and opinions (which is a very important skill to have in English).

Use a checklist when asking the child to write in a specific genre, so they know exactly what needs to be included in their work to make it successful. The checklist will also encourage the child to develop their independence, as once they have completed the task, they can then self-evaluate their work.

Newspaper article	
Features of a newspaper article	Tick when included
Headline	
Byline	
Introductory paragraph	
Main body of text	
Quotes	
Pictures	
Captions	

When introducing children to a writing genre for the first time, it may be necessary to do the activity as a group, so children get a clear idea of what they are being asked to do. If you model the way grammar and punctuation can be used to make writing more exciting, more dramatic and more formal, the child will soon start to develop their own style of writing. It may also benefit the children if they are given a reason to write; in Key Stage 1 the children may write a letter to Father Christmas, or a list of questions for a book character to answer. However, in Key Stage 2, writing can be linked to a book the children are reading. For instance, children could write a newspaper article to appeal for a missing character; a report about an animal they have researched; or a diary entry to detail how the character would have felt during a particular event or time period.

Spelling, punctuation and grammar (SPaG)

Since the new curriculum was introduced in September 2014, one of the elements of an English lesson is now spelling, punctuation and grammar. I know what you are thinking: these skills have always been part of an English lesson. You are right, they have; but now the teaching of them is far more explicit. Therefore, as part of an English session, it may be necessary for you to work alongside a small group of children in the classroom to develop their understanding and the importance of using the correct spellings, punctuation and grammar throughout their writing. At first, you may find yourself constantly reminding the children to use capital letters, full stops and finger spaces (but it will all be worth it in the end, when they start to use these independently).

Tips

Tip 1: Offer the parents the opportunity to come into school and work alongside their child, so they have a chance to see how the curriculum has changed, the expectations that are placed on the child, and practical ways they can support their child at home.

Tip 2: Give the children a paragraph that contains a range of small punctuation errors. The children can then (using a highlighter) identify which punctuation has been missed out or used incorrectly. *Using the IWB to add and remove punctuation and grammatical errors can make the lesson a lot more fun and interactive, which, as always, can promote a lot of 'interesting' discussions.

Tip 3: Produce punctuation fans, so the children can quickly show which punctuation has been missed out of a pre-prepared paragraph. *This is a quick and easy way to assess whether the children have understood the topic taught and who may require more support.

Tip 4: Have a range of key words (or 'high frequency' words) displayed around the classroom, so children can refer to them as and when needed. Try to put these words into 'word families' to give the children the opportunity to look for spelling patterns in words and make links between words:

The 'ought' word family	The 'aught' word family
bought	caught
brought	fraught
thought	distraught
sought	daughter
nought	naughty

Tip 5: Provide the children with a 'have a go' book, which encourages them to have a go at spelling an unfamiliar word and then check it with an adult if they are still not confident about their attempt. *It is important to praise the child for the sounds in the word they have got right (even if only phonetically correct).

Tip 6: Make mistakes 'on purpose' when writing on the IWB, so children will be able to correct any mistakes made; the children will soon be saying which capital letters or full stops have been missed out, or any spelling mistakes that have been made.

Practical ideas

Make sure the child is being introduced to the correct terminology, alongside a more basic explanation depending on the ability and understanding of the child.

Use an interactive whiteboard (IWB) to help to explain any new vocabulary as and when needed; conjunctions (formerly connectives), modal verbs, adverbials of time (formerly time connectives), pronouns and subordinating clauses are just some of the new phrases the children will be expected to know and use correctly. *At this point, I strongly suggest you invest in a SPaG dictionary, which will give you definitions of what the new vocabulary means and examples of how to use it correctly.

Have dictionaries and high frequency cards on the desks, so the child can refer to them if they are unsure of the spelling or meaning of a word.

Use educational websites to introduce and reinforce the many types of punctuation there are. *At present, there are numerous websites that show children how to use punctuation effectively in a fun and interactive way; these engage even the most reluctant of learners.

Children can struggle with spelling, punctuation and grammar whatever their age and ability, to varying degrees. But having someone who is going to listen to them, work alongside them, and show them how to improve their skills effectively will make a difference not only to their academic ability, but also to their confidence.

Reading in groups (RIG) (or guided reading groups)

Over the last year, the terminology around reading has changed in some primary schools, where 'guided reading groups' are now being referred to as RIG. As part of this strategy, the whole class reads the same book (which is aimed slightly higher than the ability of the children in the class). The main aim of this strategy is to challenge the children through the questioning used during the sessions. However, there will be children who simply cannot access the text due to EAL, learning difficulties or poor comprehension skills. Therefore, it may be necessary to work with a small group of children to practise the skills needed for reading:

- Looking at the pictures, to see if there are any signs of what is going on.
- Reading around the text to look for clues in the sentence.
- Decoding words, which will eventually build up the reading fluency.

- Understanding the text (comprehension).
- Inferring (reading between the lines, working out what they think may have happened, based on what they have read).
- Using the appropriate intonation (tone of voice) when reading in the voice of different characters.

Tips

Tip 1: If a child is reluctant to read, it may be helpful to introduce them to books without words. The child, with the support of a small group (and you, of course), can think about: what has happened in the story; what could happen in the story; the names of the characters; and whether the story has a positive or negative ending. *Talking about a story in a fun way sometimes gives the child that little bit of extra confidence needed to read aloud in a small group situation, as it can take away the stress of getting stuck or struggling over a word and getting laughed at (as all of the children in the group are in the same boat).

Tip 2: Make sure the book is appropriate for the child (too easy and the child will get bored; too hard and the child will not develop a love of reading).

Tip 3: Give every child a chance to read, even the most reluctant readers. Teach the other children how to create a supportive environment: listening to each other, never laughing at each other and helping each other when you can see someone is struggling are just some of the ways the group can encourage a child who may be shy or lacking in confidence when being asked to read aloud.

Tip 4: Stop reading every so often to check the children have understood what has been read, by asking who the main characters are; what important events have happened; why the events happened; and whether there were any problems that needed to be resolved.

Tip 5: Ask the children to look at the front cover of the book and get them to make a prediction about what the story might be about, what might happen to the characters, and what may happen at the end of the story.

Tip 6: Ask lots of questions about why the children think something has happened: Why do you think the character chose to do that? All of the 'why do you think?' questions help to develop the important skill of inference. Children need to be able to put themselves into someone else's situation and say how they may feel if faced with the same issue as the character.

Tip 7: Ask the children a question about a piece of text they have just finished reading. Get the children to find out where in the text the answer to your question is. This skill will help the children during SATs assessments (in Year 2 and Year 6).

Tip 8: Give children time to work out unfamiliar words; do not be too quick to jump in and help them. Encourage the child to use their reading strategies to: work out the word; sound out the word using their phonological knowledge; break the word into smaller chunks; and look for a familiar word within the word (this way the child will at least be confident when reading some of the words).

Practical ideas

Photocopy texts that are being read in RIG group, so children can highlight important events in the text and words they do not understand. *The children can then practise their dictionary skills when looking up the unfamiliar words in a purposeful way, rather than just being given a random word to look up.

Use the IWB to show the children pictures of time periods such as Victorians and Tudors, e.g. objects from different eras, such as Victorian bedpans or World War II Spitfire aeroplanes. By showing the children what is meant by these words, the child will be able to build up a better picture of what they have just read.

Encourage the child to use highlighter pens so the child can show where they have found the correct answer, in preparation for their reading assessments (in Year 2 and Year 6).

Anger management groups

There may be times during the day when a child enters the setting or the classroom in an angry or distressed state. Throughout Chapter 4, I have included many strategies that can be used to calm a situation down and consequences that may need to be given if a child makes the wrong choices. Although both can work for a short time, I have learnt over the years just how important it is to teach the children the importance of being able to self-regulate and manage their own feelings and behaviour (by being able to spot the warnings signs before the child reaches the point of losing their temper).

However, before you start any groups of this nature, I strongly suggest training is sought, as running this type of group is not only quite specialised, but can also be stressful at times. But you do not need to worry; the setting will arrange all of the training and support needed. The training will provide an overview of what can trigger anger in children, the strategies that can be used to help calm a situation and ways the child can be taught to self-regulate their feelings. As well as training, it may be necessary to talk to the SENDCo, who will be able to provide some previous background on the types of interventions that have been tried previously, what has been successful in the past, and which strategies have simply not worked at all.

Although some of the issues that cause the child to become angry can be easily solved (such as friendship problems or finding work in the setting too hard or too easy), other issues are not so easy to sort out. (The child has been through a bereavement; parents have separated; or the child has been subjected to or witnessed abuse or domestic violence.) Whatever situation the child is facing, there are strategies that can be used to help the child calm down or manage their feelings appropriately:

Calming down

- Blowing bubbles (as silly as it sounds) can really help to calm a child down, as it is impossible to stay angry whilst they are concentrating on blowing the biggest bubble. (I was given this tip by a play therapist I used to work with.)

- Taking deep breaths, counting to ten on the breath in and counting to ten as they breathe out can be a really quick and effective way to help the child to calm down, as they have to focus on their breathing, rather than on the issue that made them angry in the first place.

- Provide the child with a safe place to go if they feel they are beginning to feel angry or upset. Having a designated space will give the child some much-needed time away from other children (which may sometimes be all that is needed). *This may just be the reading area, which often has pillows for the children to lie down on.

- Have a range of 'calming down' activities available, should a child just need some 'time out'. Activities that I have found to be useful with children include colouring in, construction toys, and whiteboard and pens (where the child can write down how they are feeling, with the opportunity to rub out offending words once they have got them out their system).

- Organise for the child to have access to a listening centre if they start to feel stressed, so they can listen to calming music, which can help them to block out any noises that are causing them to become distressed.

- Take the child to a place where distractions and stimulation are kept to a minimum (neutral colours, reduced lighting and nothing on the walls). *Many settings at present are lucky enough to have a sensory room; if this is not the case, it may be necessary to take the child to another area of the setting: the canteen, library or PPA room, or any other quiet place in the setting (this can be extremely difficult in a busy primary setting, but you will find somewhere eventually; it may just take a while).

Managing feelings

- Use role-play scenarios that give the child the opportunity to practise how to react to certain situations and how they may need to change the way they react, in order for it to be appropriate.

- Use puppets, so the child or group can act out their thoughts and feelings. Often, talking about an experience or feeling in the third person can help the child to express themselves more when talking about a 'friend'.

- Give the child the opportunity to talk about their feelings (formally, during anger management groups, and informally, if and when needed), by giving the child a time-out pass, which can be used by the child to remove themselves from a situation in which the child can feel themselves getting angry or upset.

- Play lots of games where the child can practise how to name their feelings and what could be done to alleviate those feelings.

- Provide the language to help children explain when they are beginning to feel angry or upset by something, so the child can see that other children have similar feelings.

- Have plenty of opportunities for the child to explain how they feel when they begin to feel angry. *It may be necessary for you to say how you know you are close to feeling angry or upset (you get a knot in your stomach or start to stutter and struggle to talk).

- Provide the child with a feelings diary, so the child is able to record how they are feeling, when they were feeling like this, and what has made them angry.

During the groups, there will be times when a child is describing their feelings and beginning to get frustrated with themselves. At this point, it is important to reassure the child and let them know it is okay to get angry; it is a normal response to something that they find upsetting. However, the child needs to understand there are appropriate ways to respond to things that upset them; it is not appropriate to go from 'nought to ten' at the flick of a switch.

During any given day, there may be many reasons why a child may feel angry; another child may have sworn at them, said something about a family member, or laughed at their attempts at work, to name but a few. However, the group activities can help teach the children strategies that may allow them to think of other ways they can react to a difficult situation:

- don't respond to whatever it is that makes them angry (ignore it)
- remove themselves from the situation (walk away)
- tell an adult who can help sort the issue out.

Practical ideas

Model appropriate behaviour to the children at all times (although this may not always be possible; we are only human after all). *The children are very intuitive and will be quick to pick up how you are feeling, whether you are feeling happy, sad or angry about a particular situation. This works both ways, as you will be able to tell how they are feeling, once you have got to know the children in the setting.

Send the child to other classrooms to give a message (pre-warn the teacher and TA before sending the child, to make sure the child gets a positive response).

Praise the child when you see the child make the right decision or right choice (e.g. the child walking away from a situation that may have previously caused the child to get into an argument or physical fight, or the child asking an adult to help them sort out an issue that is troubling them).

Ask parents and members of staff to watch out for (and note down) occasions when the child has made a good choice when dealing with a situation or person that normally causes an issue.

Be positive and teach children in the class the language of positivity.

Tips

Tip 1: Always ask parents for written permission for any interventions that are offered to the child.

Tip 2: Always make sure you 'catch the child' doing something positive, and make a comment on the good choice that has been made. Remember: the child needs to know what they have done 'right'.

Tip 3: Introduce the children in the setting to positive and consistent ways of dealing with issues that may cause the child to become upset; providing alternative thinking strategies (PATHS) is a programme that encourages the child to develop communication skills, problem-solving skills and an awareness of how their actions affect both themselves and others.

Tip 4: Make sure you have a person with whom you can talk when you have had to deal with a particularly difficult child or situation. (Don't worry; we all need to rant at some point or other.)

Self-esteem

Often, you will find that children who have anger issues also have poor self-esteem. The child may feel everything is their fault, that they get the blame for everything, and that everyone in the setting is against them and is always trying to get them into trouble. However, in order for the child to overcome this, it may be necessary to introduce the children to activities that can build confidence and develop their sense of worth, as part of the anger management sessions.

- Use collage to celebrate what makes a child unique, using words and pictures to represent the good qualities the child has: 'happy', 'friendly', 'helpful', 'sporty' and 'generous' are just some of the positive attributes that can be highlighted.

- Ask the child to design a 'coat of arms' or giant initial letter of their name, which can be illustrated either with pictures that represent what the child feels they are like as a person, or with hobbies and interests they enjoy in their spare time (e.g. shopping, gaming and reading, to name but a few).

- Provide the child with a notebook, so they can record any positive experiences they have had at home or at school; the child can then refer back to them if they are going through a difficult time and feeling sad or down.

- Organise a nurture group, where a child with low self-esteem may work alongside a small group of children who can model appropriate behaviour to the child: how to speak to each other kindly and make meaningful, long-lasting friendships.

- Use lots of positive praise whenever you see the child doing something 'good'. The child might have tried hard to complete work, answered a question in a whole-class situation, used their best handwriting, or simply followed an instruction first time. By doing this, the child will know that you have noticed them and are 'proud' of their achievements, which can have a massive impact on the child and their self-esteem.

- Introduce a 'child of the day' or 'VIP' child, where a child from the class receives compliments from the rest of the children in the class (normally at the end of the school day), and where children practise giving and receiving positive praise.

Initially, when groups are first introduced, the children may be reluctant to leave the classroom through fear of the unknown. But if you involve the children in the planning process and base the group around the child's interests, they are far more likely to participate in the sessions. By making the activities fun, the children can learn a whole range of skills (not just academic), which they simply would not be able to learn in a whole-class situation (it is just up to you now to think of weird and wacky ways to engage the children).

When supporting small groups of children (whatever the needs of the children) it can sometimes be stressful, especially if the progress of the children seems to be slow. However, if you ever start to feel downhearted, you might try a technique that I use a lot. Take a look at the photos and work the child produced at the start of the year and compare it to what they are doing now. I guarantee the difference will be amazing (and you will have played a huge part in the progress). I know it sounds silly, but it is easy to overlook progress when you are with the child every day; so take a minute (yes, a whole minute) out of your day to see the child changing in front of your very eyes.

Final story

Over the years I have supported many children in a variety of ways, but it is always lovely when previous students come back into the setting or approach me as I am going about my daily business (usually when doing my weekly shop) to tell me what a positive impact I had on their life and how I inspired them to work hard and achieve. Being told this by a child you have worked with (even though they are now in their late teens or early twenties) is a very humbling experience and one of the many reasons I love my job.

Well, you have finally reached the end of the book, and I do hope it was everything you expected it to be. I have tried to be as honest as I can about the roles and responsibilities you may have when you take on the role of a TA in a primary setting. (I hope I have not put you off doing the job.) I have also tried to give you a range of activities and practical ideas that can be used with all children, whatever their age, ability and need. The main aim of writing this book was to pass on what a joy it is to work with children and support them to reach their full potential (whatever this may be), and to inspire you not just to be a good teaching assistant, but to be an outstanding teaching assistant – one who encourages all children to become lifelong learners.

Glossary of abbreviations and acronyms

ADHD	Attention deficit hyperactivity disorder
ARE	Age-related expectations
ASD	Autistic spectrum disorder
BECo	Behaviour coordinator
Below ARE	Below age-related expectations
BSL	British Sign Language
BTE	Behind-the-ear hearing aids
CA	Classroom assistant
CAMHS	Child and Adolescent Mental Health Services
CAT Team	Communication and autism team
CEOP	Child Exploitation and Online Protection Centre
CP	Child protection
CPA	Concrete, pictorial and abstract
CPD	Continued professional development
DSL	Designated safeguarding lead
DSP	Designated safeguarding person
DT	Design technology
DV	Domestic violence
EAL	English as an additional language
ECHP	Education, care and health plan
Ed Psych	Educational psychologist
ERIC	Everyone reading in groups

FGM   Female genital mutilation

G and T   Gifted and talented

HLTA   Higher level teaching assistant

IBP   Individual behaviour plan
IEP   Individual education plan
ITE   In-the-ear hearing aids
IWB   Interactive whiteboard

KS1   Key Stage 1
KS2   Key Stage 2

LM   Learning mentor
LSA   Learning support assistant

MASH   Multi-agency safeguarding hub

OCD   Obsessive compulsive disorder
ODD   Oppositional defiant disorder
OFSTED   Office for Standards in Education, Children's Services and
          Skills

PATHS   Promoting alternative thinking strategies
P.E.   Physical education
PPA   Planning, preparation and assessment
PSHE   Personal, social and health education
PSS   Pupil support services

RIG   Reading in groups

SALT   Speech and language therapist
SEAL   Social and emotional aspects of learning
SEN   Special educational needs
SENCo   Special educational needs coordinator
SEND   Special educational needs and disability
SENDCo   Special educational needs and disability coordinator

SIG	Social interaction group
SLT	Senior leadership team
SMT	Senior management team
SPaG	Spelling, punctuation and grammar
TA	Teaching assistant

Index